Practicing for Today's Tests

FOR KIDS

Level **3** Language Arts

Author
Jennifer Prior

Introduction Author

Delia E. Racines, Ph.D.
Faculty, University of Southern California
USC Language Academy

Publishing Credits

Corinne Burton, M.A.Ed., *President*;
Emily R. Smith, M.A.Ed., *Editorial Director*;
Debra J. Housel, M.S.Ed., *Editor*; Jennifer Wilson,
Editor; Courtney Patterson, *Multimedia Designer*;
Stephanie Bernard, *Assistant Editor*;
Monique Dominguez, *Production Artist*

Image Credits

p. 66: iStock; All other images from Shutterstock unless noted otherwise.

Standards

© Copyright 2010. National Governors Association Center for Best Practices and
Council of Chief State School Officers. All rights reserved.

Shell Education

5301 Oceanus Drive
Huntington Beach, CA 92649-1030
http://www.shelleducation.com
ISBN 978-1-4258-1436-6
© 2015 Shell Educational Publishing, Inc.

Table of Contents

Today's Next Generation Tests

> "To be college and career ready, students must now read across a broad range of high-quality texts from diverse cultures and times in history."
>
> —Delia E. Racines, Ph.D.

Education is currently undergoing a dramatic shift when it comes to the ways we measure and assess for learning. Educational standards across the nation are designed to provide clear and meaningful goals for our students. These standards serve as a frame of reference for educators, parents, and students and are most critical when decisions must be made about curriculum, textbooks, assessments, and other aspects of instructional programs (Conley 2014). Part of the disconnect with standards in the recent past has been the vast differences and lack of consistency in expectations that became a major concern for the quality of education students were receiving across the country (Conley 2014; Wiley and Wright 2004).

Standards in education in the United States are not a new concept. However, the role of educational standards has recently shifted to not only ensure that all students have access to equitable education no matter where they live, but also to ensure a more consistent national expectation for what all students should know to be successful in a rapidly changing economy and society (Kornhaber, Griffith, and Tyler 2014).

Scales, scores, and assessments are absolutely necessary to ascertain the current status of students. This kind of data is vital for teachers to understand what is missing and what the next steps should be. The real question about assessment isn't whether we should assess but rather what kinds of assessments should be used. Along with the current shift to more consistent and rigorous standards, states now measure student progress with assessments that require higher-order thinking skills necessary for preparation for college and/or careers.

So, what is this new yardstick that is being used? How is it better than yardsticks of the past? And how do we best prepare students to be measured with this yardstick in a way that tells the whole story? The next generation tests intend to provide results that are comparable across all states and will use more performance-based tasks as well as technology-enhanced items. This is very different in comparison to the standardized testing that teachers, students, and parents are used to (National Governors Association Center for Best Practices 2010; Rothman 2013).

The following descriptions serve as explanations of how the three most prominent next-generation tests are different from assessments of the past.

Today's Next Generation Tests *(cont.)*

Partnership for Assessment of Readiness for College and Careers (PARCC)

The PARCC assessment is a common set of computer-based, K–12 assessments in English language arts and mathematics. These assessments replace previous state tests in grades 3–11 used to meet the requirements of the Elementary and Secondary Education Act (PARCC 2013). The most significant difference in the PARCC tests is the use of performance tasks that ask students to apply their knowledge to solve extended problems rather than simply regurgitate answers (Rothman 2013).

PARCC consists of four assessments a year. The two optional assessments include diagnostic assessments (in reading, writing, and mathematics) that may be administered at the beginning of each school year and as mid-year assessments to help predict students' likely end-of-year performances.

The two required summative assessments consist of a performance task and an end-of-year test for each grade. Previously, in English language arts, many states did not assess writing and few assessed critical-thinking skills. The PARCC assessment does both. The performance-based assessment is in English language arts and mathematics and includes asking students to analyze literature as well as narrative writing tasks. Students also take the end-of-year assessments in English language arts and mathematics. The results of the two tests are combined to determine the summative assessment score (PARCC 2013). Lastly, a separate speaking and listening component is required and can be administered anytime during the academic year. The results of the speaking and listening component are not be combined with the other assessments to determine students' summative assessment scores.

Many of today's standardized tests are administered online.

Today's Next Generation Tests *(cont.)*

Smarter Balanced Assessment Consortium (SBAC)

The SBAC is also developing summative assessments in English language arts and mathematics. Their assessments have two major components: performance tasks and an end-of-the-year computer adaptive test. Computer adaptive tests mean that questions are adjusted based on students' previous responses. These two major components are administered during the last 12 weeks of the school year (SBAC 2014). The computer adaptive test feature, which is the biggest difference from the PARCC, is intended to enable administrators and teachers to use results within weeks to more efficiently and quickly identify students' ability levels in an effort to differentiate instruction. The SBAC assessments go beyond multiple-choice tests to include short constructed responses, extended constructed responses, and performance tasks. These allow students to complete in-depth projects that demonstrate both analytical skills and real-world problem solving (SBAC 2014). Performance tasks are online in reading, writing, and mathematics and may also be administered as part of the optional interim assessments throughout the year. Results will be available within weeks after a student completes a performance task.

State of Texas Assessment of Academic Readiness (STAAR®)

The STAAR® replaced the Texas Assessment of Knowledge and Skills (TAKS). It was developed and adopted by the Texas School Board of Education within the Texas Education Agency. This assessment focuses on readiness for college and/or careers with test questions that focus on rigor and critical analysis.

For elementary school and middle school, the tests cover the same subjects and grades as the previous state testing program, the TAKS. The most significant differences between the TAKS and the STAAR® are apparent at the high school level with 12 end-of-course assessments that focus on fewer skills in a deeper manner and replace previous grade-specific tests (Texas Education Agency 2014). The STAAR® assesses the Texas Essential Knowledge and Skills. However, there are a greater number of items with higher cognitive demands. In writing, students are required to write two essays instead of one.

Categories of Questions

In order for students today to be better prepared for college and/or careers, they must be able to read widely and deeply across a range of informational and literary texts (National Governors Association Center for Best Practices 2010). In today's standards, there are often three categories of reading standards. On assessments, these categories are represented by three categories of questions. The questions include new terminology that defines specific skills and understandings that all students must demonstrate. **Note:** See *Appendix B* (pages 100–103) for how these categories are represented in each practice exercise in this book.

Overall, today's college and career readiness reading standards depict the picture of what students should be able to exhibit with increasing proficiency and on a regular basis. To be college and career ready, students must now read across a broad range of high-quality texts from diverse cultures and times in history. The reading standards emphasize the skills necessary to critically read and continuously make connections among ideas and texts. Students also learn to distinguish poor reasoning as well as ambiguities in texts. The following explanation of the terms related to each of the three reading categories will better prepare educators and parents for today's tests.

Key Ideas and Details

This category stresses the importance of understanding specific information in various texts. Overall, students must be able to identify specific details and then gain deeper meaning from what is read. Specifically, this category requires students to be able to do the following things.

Students should be able to . . .	To show how they know this, students must . . .
read text closely to really understand what it says.	identify specific details from the text.
make conclusions based on what they identify from a text.	say or write specific details to support their conclusions.
determine the main idea or theme from a text and analyze its development.	identify and summarize key supporting details that support the theme or main idea.
figure out how and why individuals, events, or ideas develop and interact over the course of a text.	explain details about how characters and/or the story develop at different times throughout the text from the beginning to the end.

Categories of Questions *(cont.)*

Craft and Structure

This category stresses the importance of being able to identify patterns of various text structures to more easily synthesize and summarize information. Physical text structures (captions, pictures, diagrams, italicized print, bold print, etc.) are purposely used in texts to organize different types of information. This is true for both fiction and nonfiction texts. Specifically, this category requires students to be able to do the following things.

Students should be able to . . .	To show how they know this, students must . . .
interpret words and phrases as they are used in technical, connotative, or figurative texts.	explain the purposes of different types of texts and distinguish what kinds of words or phrases are used in each type.
analyze how specific word choices shape meaning or tone.	identify and explain why certain words are used and how different words alter the feelings readers experience from texts.
analyze the parts or structures of a text.	identify the names and purposes of each different structure within a text.
explain the relationships between parts or structures within a text.	explain how sentences, paragraphs, and larger portions of texts relate to one another and the whole text.
figure out how point of view shapes the content and style of a text.	explain how different perspectives could change the meaning of a text.
figure out how purpose changes the content and style of a text.	explain how different purposes could alter the meaning of a text.

Categories of Questions *(cont.)*

Integration of Knowledge and Ideas

This category stresses the importance of being able to understand the main idea of texts and analyze details presented in various formats. Students should then be able to draw conclusions based on the text, interpret the purpose and structure of texts, and apply the meaning across other texts and knowledge. In general, students should compare and contrast texts and ultimately increase comprehensibility of more complex texts. Specifically, this category requires students to be able to do the following things.

Students should be able to . . .	To show how they know this, students must . . .
evaluate content presented in various formats (e.g., in writing, visually, via media, and numerically).	describe what they understand about the content through various formats.
integrate or put together cross-curricular content that is presented in different formats.	explain how ideas presented in various formats are related to one another.
outline what the argument is in a text.	identify specific claims in a text that include how valid the reasoning is in the argument, how relevant the reasoning is to the argument, and whether there is enough evidence to support the argument.
analyze how two or more texts address similar themes or topics to build knowledge or to compare the approaches the authors take.	identify themes of multiple texts and then describe similarities and differences between the texts.
compare the approaches different authors take.	identify the approaches different authors take and then describe similarities and differences between them.

Making It Meaningful

The section has been included to make this book's test practice more meaningful. The purpose of this section is to provide sample guiding questions framed around a specific practice exercise. This will serve as a meaningful and real-life application of the test practice. Each of the guiding questions serves as a thinking prompt to ensure that the three categories of the reading standards have been considered. The guiding questions may be used with students as a teacher-led think aloud or to individually assess how students are approaching and understanding complex texts. The framework used in this model serves as a template for how to approach other fiction and nonfiction texts. The template supports educators in preparing students for today's tests and helps make meaning of the reading standards to ultimately ensure that the learning becomes more meaningful for all students.

Begin with the Craft and Structure reading standards in mind by asking students these questions:

What type of text is this?

What is the purpose of this type of text?

Identify what text structures are used in this text and why.

What is the relationship among certain vocabulary words?

How do the words shape the tone?

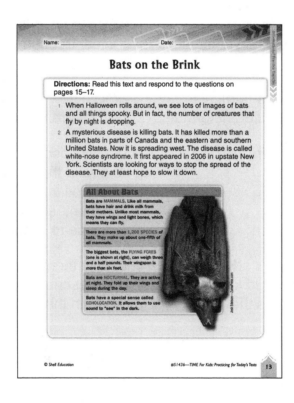

Then, with the Key Ideas and Details reading standards in mind, coach students to do the following:

Underline the key details you have noticed so far.

Write a summary sentence with these details as support.

List or create a timeline of important events in the character's story.

Finally, check for understanding with the Integration of Knowledge and Ideas reading standards in mind by asking students to do the following:

Make connections across other content areas.

Explain how varied ideas relate to one another.

Making It Meaningful (cont.)

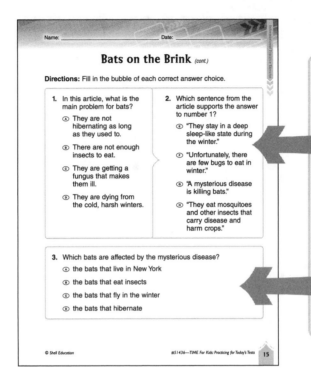

For all questions, students should do the following:

"Ask yourself what the directions are asking you to do. Do you need to analyze, infer, evaluate, formulate, describe, support, explain, summarize, compare, contrast, predict, fill in, complete, etc.?"

When answers refer to specific sentences in the text, guide students in the following way:

"These answers reference specific sentences in the text. Go back and find these sentences. Then, reread the text around the sentences to find out which one is the answer to the question."

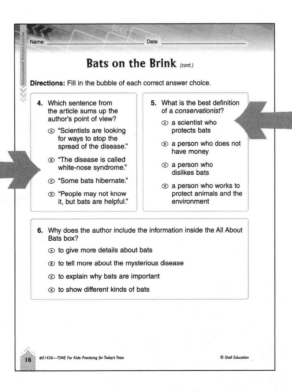

When students are asked vocabulary questions, help them in the following way:

"Find the specific vocabulary word in the text and circle it. Use the other words around it to figure out its meaning using context clues."

Making It Meaningful (cont.)

When students have to use the text to defend their answers, guide them in the following way:

"Find the specific quoted statement in the text. Underline specific details in the text that support this statement and your response to the prompt."

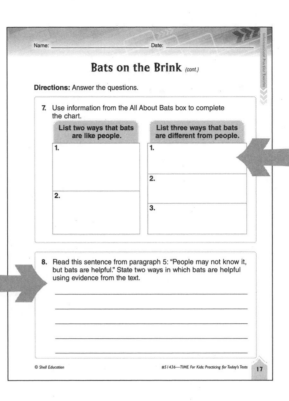

If students need to complete graphic organizers, use guiding questions to help them determine how the text can help them respond.

"What does the chart say about bats being like people? Go back to the text in the chart and use it to answer the question."

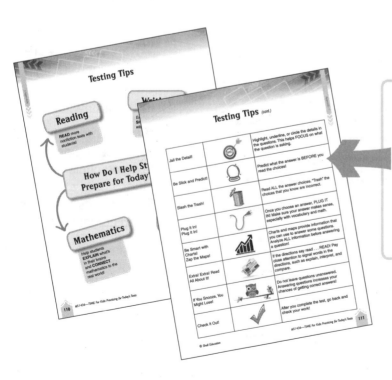

To support students in preparing for today's tests, send home the Testing Tips flyers on pages 110–111. There is one page intended to guide parents in how to prepare their children and a second page to help students understand ways they can be more succssful while taking tests.

Name: _____   Date: _____

Bats on the Brink

Directions: Read this text and respond to the questions on pages 15–17.

1   When Halloween rolls around, we see lots of images of bats and all things spooky. But in fact, the number of creatures that fly by night is dropping.

2   A mysterious disease is killing bats. It has killed more than a million bats in parts of Canada and the eastern and southern United States. Now it is spreading west. The disease is called white-nose syndrome. It first appeared in 2006 in upstate New York. Scientists are looking for ways to stop the spread of the disease. They at least hope to slow it down.

All About Bats

Bats are MAMMALS. Like all mammals, bats have hair and drink milk from their mothers. Unlike most mammals, they have wings and light bones, which means they can fly.

There are more than 1,200 SPECIES of bats. They make up about one-fifth of all mammals.

The biggest bats, the FLYING FOXES (one is shown at right), can weigh three and a half pounds. Their wingspan is more than six feet.

Bats are NOCTURNAL. They are active at night. They fold up their wings and sleep during the day.

Bats have a special sense called ECHOLOCATION. It allows them to use sound to "see" in the dark.

Josh Edelson—ZumaPress.com

Bats on the Brink (cont.)

Saving the Species

3   Some bats hibernate. They stay in a deep sleep-like state during the winter. Only hibernating bats seem to get white-nose syndrome. Scientists think that the disease is caused by a fungus. The fungus grows on a bat's nose, wings, and ears. It hurts wing tissues. It may make the bats uncomfortable. That causes them to end their hibernation early. When they do, they burn up fat stored in their bodies. Bats need it to survive the winter. Unfortunately, there are few bugs to eat in winter. With nothing to eat, many of the bats starve.

4   Researchers are testing drugs to fight the fungus. They told TIME For Kids that more money is needed. The money would be used to study the disease and find a cure. "It's important to save bats," says scientist Mollie Matteson. "They are fascinating animals. We can learn a lot from them."

5   People may not know it, but bats are helpful. They eat mosquitoes and other insects that carry disease and harm crops. "Bats are our friends," says bat expert Tom Kunz. "They help people and the environment they live in."

Name: _____   Date: _____

Bats on the Brink (cont.)

Directions: Fill in the bubble of each correct answer choice.

1. In this article, what is the main problem for bats?

   Ⓐ They are not hibernating as long as they used to.

   Ⓑ There are not enough insects to eat.

   Ⓒ They are getting a fungus that makes them ill.

   Ⓓ They are dying from the cold, harsh winters.

2. Which sentence from the article supports the answer to number 1?

   Ⓔ "They stay in a deep sleep-like state during the winter."

   Ⓕ "Unfortunately, there are few bugs to eat in winter."

   Ⓖ "A mysterious disease is killing bats."

   Ⓗ "They eat mosquitoes and other insects that carry disease and harm crops."

3. Which bats are affected by the mysterious disease?

   Ⓐ the bats that live in New York

   Ⓑ the bats that eat insects

   Ⓒ the bats that fly in the winter

   Ⓓ the bats that hibernate

Name: _____   Date: _____

Bats on the Brink (cont.)

Directions: Fill in the bubble of each correct answer choice.

4. Which sentence from the article sums up the author's point of view?

   Ⓐ "Scientists are looking for ways to stop the spread of the disease."

   Ⓑ "The disease is called white-nose syndrome."

   Ⓒ "Some bats hibernate."

   Ⓓ "People may not know it, but bats are helpful."

5. What is the best definition of a *conservationist*?

   Ⓐ a scientist who protects bats

   Ⓑ a person who does not have money

   Ⓒ a person who dislikes bats

   Ⓓ a person who works to protect animals and the environment

6. Why does the author include the information inside the All About Bats box?

   Ⓐ to give more details about bats

   Ⓑ to tell more about the mysterious disease

   Ⓒ to explain why bats are important

   Ⓓ to show different kinds of bats

Bats on the Brink (cont.)

Directions: Answer the questions.

7. Use information from the All About Bats box to complete the chart.

List two ways that bats are like people.	List three ways that bats are different from people.
1.	1.
	2.
2.	3.

8. Read this sentence from paragraph 5: "People may not know it, but bats are helpful." State two ways in which bats are helpful using evidence from the text.

_____

_____

_____

_____

_____

Name: _____   Date: _____

The Scoop on Sugar

Directions: Read this text and respond to the questions on pages 21–23.

1   Can you imagine eating 20 teaspoons of sugar? Does that sound gross? The typical American kid gets that much sugar each day.

2   A recent report said kids get about 16 percent of their calories from sugar that has been added to food. "It's too much," says Dr. David Katz. He's a nutrition expert at Yale University. "It's one of the major problems with our diet," he told TIME For Kids.

3   Some of that sugar comes from foods like candy, soda, and cereal. You expect them to be sweet. But much of the sugar that kids eat is hidden. Food companies add sugar to lots of things, from ketchup to crackers. "There are pasta sauces that have more added sugar than ice-cream toppings," says Katz.

4   As a result, people get used to eating very sweet foods. "If you soak taste buds in sugar all day long, they just get used to it," Katz says. "Everything needs to be highly sweetened to be satisfying."

Cut the Sugar

5   Most kids know that eating too much sugar is not healthy. Sugar can cause cavities. And filling up on sweets means not eating more nutritious foods. Some experts think that eating too much sugar can also lead to serious health problems.

6   Three scientists have called on the government to help people eat less sugar. They want to ban the sale of sugary drinks to kids. They want to keep sugary foods out of schools. And they want to add taxes to heavily sweetened foods. "We need to unsweeten our lives," Dr. Robert Lustig, one of the scientists, told TIME For Kids.

The Scoop on Sugar (cont.)

Expand Your Choices

7 We need food to live. It should help keep us healthy. Now we're learning our food may be doing the opposite. Perhaps someday the changes scientists want will happen. In the meantime, what can you do to cut down on extra sugar? Changing our eating habits isn't easy. We like the foods we like. The good news is, you don't have to give up your favorite cereal or soda completely. The key is to find balance.

8 First, look at the ingredients list on food packages. Packages may use different names for sugar. Ingredients that end in *ose* are sugars. Sucrose and fructose are two examples. The word *syrup* means it's a sugar, too.

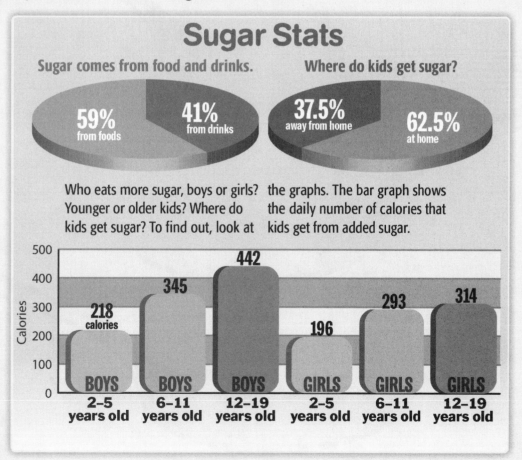

Sugar Stats

Sugar comes from food and drinks.

59% from foods

41% from drinks

Where do kids get sugar?

37.5% away from home

62.5% at home

Who eats more sugar, boys or girls? Younger or older kids? Where do kids get sugar? To find out, look at the graphs. The bar graph shows the daily number of calories that kids get from added sugar.

218 calories	345	442	196	293	314
BOYS	BOYS	BOYS	GIRLS	GIRLS	GIRLS
2–5 years old	6–11 years old	12–19 years old	2–5 years old	6–11 years old	12–19 years old

Calories (y-axis: 0, 100, 200, 300, 400, 500)

The Scoop on Sugar *(cont.)*

9 Second, try new things! Replace some of those sugary foods with ones that don't have added sugar. Expand your choices. You'll find lots of different foods that also taste great.

10 Dr. Lustig says to eat natural foods such as fresh fruits and vegetables. Stay away from processed foods. "Eat real food," he says. "Food that came out of the ground or animals that ate food that came out of the ground." Now that's food for thought.

Name: _____   Date: _____

The Scoop on Sugar *(cont.)*

Directions: Fill in the bubble of each correct answer choice.

1. What change does the author suggest the reader make?

   Ⓐ Eat a balance of healthy foods and sugary foods.

   Ⓑ Stop eating sugar.

   Ⓒ Only eat fruits and vegetables.

   Ⓓ Don't eat pasta sauce.

2. Which sentence from the article supports the answer to number 1?

   Ⓔ "First, look at the ingredients list on food packages."

   Ⓕ "Food companies add sugar to lots of things, from ketchup to crackers."

   Ⓖ "Stay away from processed foods."

   Ⓗ "Replace some of those sugary foods with ones that don't have added sugar."

3. How much sugar does the average American kid eat daily?

   Ⓐ 2 teaspoons

   Ⓑ 16 teaspoons

   Ⓒ 20 teaspoons

   Ⓓ 20 tablespoons

Name: _____   Date: _____

The Scoop on Sugar *(cont.)*

Directions: Fill in the bubble of each correct answer choice.

4. What is the author's main message?

   Ⓐ Eating too much sugar is bad for us.

   Ⓑ Food companies are trying to harm children.

   Ⓒ The government needs to add taxes on sugary foods.

   Ⓓ Crackers, ketchup, and pasta sauce are bad for us.

5. What is a *nutrition expert*?

   Ⓐ a person who does not like sugar

   Ⓑ a person who knows which foods are good and bad for us

   Ⓒ a scientist who studies sugar

   Ⓓ a person who works for the government

6. Why does the author include the Sugar Stats graph?

   Ⓐ to prove that sugary foods do not always taste sweet

   Ⓑ to show which foods contain the most sugar

   Ⓒ to prove that most kids eat sugar away from home

   Ⓓ to show who is eating sugar at various ages

Name: _____   Date: _____

The Scoop on Sugar *(cont.)*

Directions: Answer the questions.

7. Write a paragraph telling how you can change your diet to reduce the amount of sugar you eat. Include at least two ideas from the article in your paragraph.

_____

_____

_____

_____

_____

8. Complete the graphic organizer with food items mentioned in the article.

Foods That Contain Too Much Sugar	Foods That Are Better For You

Name: _____   Date: _____

A Woman Up a Tree

Directions: Read this text and respond to the questions on pages 26–28.

1 Julia "Butterfly" Hill is a woman who lives her beliefs. Like real butterflies, Hill has spent a lot of time up in the air. For two years, she lived in the branches of a redwood tree. In 1997, Hill climbed the 200-foot-tall tree as a protest. She wanted to stop loggers from cutting down redwood trees in northern California. She said, "Here I can be the voice and face of this tree."

2 It was a tough two years for Hill. At last her sacrifice paid off. She came down after a lumber company said it wouldn't touch the 1,000-year-old giant.

3 Just a year later, the tree was in danger again. In 2000 someone cut deep into the tree's trunk with a chain saw. No one was ever caught. But the cut made the tree weak and unstable.

4 Experts fear it could be blown over by strong winter storms. Recently, Hill visited the tree, which she named Luna. She touched the 32-inch gash and said, "I feel this vicious attack on Luna as if the chain saw was going through me."

5 Hill feels strongly about the tree. When she came down from it after two years, she was sad: "I just felt like my heart was being ripped out." She added, "That tree was the best friend I've ever had." While on Luna, Hill lived in a 6-foot by 8-foot tree house. She had no shower. Friends sent up food in buckets. She cooked the food on a small gas-burning stove. She kept in shape by climbing the branches of the 18-story-high tree.

Julia "Butterfly" Hill checks the braces holding up the tree.

Shaun Walker/Eureka Times-Standard/AP

A Woman Up a Tree (cont.)

6 Hill spent most of her time in the tree talking on a cell phone. For six to eight hours a day, she gave interviews. She explained what she was doing to school students. She got about 300 letters each week from people all over the world. Most mentioned how much Hill inspired them by helping Luna.

7 Luna survived the nasty cut. An emergency team put steel braces over the gash. They did this to support the tree. It looks like the tree will live. Hill belongs to an environmental group. It is called Circle of Life Foundation. It is working with experts to figure out how to save the tree permanently.

Experts reach around the giant tree to measure the damage.

Shaun Walker/Eureka Times-Standard/AP

A Woman Up a Tree (cont.)

Directions: Fill in the bubble of each correct answer choice.

1. Why did Hill spend two years in the tree?

   Ⓐ She wanted to save it from being cut down.

   Ⓑ She liked being up off the ground.

   Ⓒ She wished she could be a butterfly.

   Ⓓ She was homeless.

2. Which statement by Hill best supports the answer to number 1?

   Ⓔ "I feel this vicious attack on Luna as if the chain saw was going through me."

   Ⓕ "Here I can be the voice and face of this tree."

   Ⓖ "That tree was the best friend I've ever had."

   Ⓗ "I just felt like my heart was being ripped out."

3. Why did Hill finally come down from the tree?

   Ⓐ She wanted to live in a house.

   Ⓑ Lumber companies promised not to cut it down.

   Ⓒ She thought the tree was dead.

   Ⓓ She did not like living outdoors.

A Woman Up a Tree *(cont.)*

Directions: Fill in the bubble of each correct answer choice.

4. How do you think the author feels about saving Luna?

   Ⓐ The author believes it is silly.

   Ⓑ The author believes it is hopeless.

   Ⓒ The author believes Hill should focus on the other trees in the forest.

   Ⓓ The author believes that saving the tree is a good thing.

5. Read these sentences from paragraph 2: "It was a tough two years for Hill. At last her sacrifice paid off." What does the phrase *her sacrifice paid off* mean?

   Ⓐ She managed to protect the tree.

   Ⓑ She earned money for saving the tree.

   Ⓒ She paid money to save the tree.

   Ⓓ She changed her mind about saving the tree.

6. Why does the author include photographs with the article?

   Ⓐ to show Hill's treehouse

   Ⓑ to show Hill living in the tree

   Ⓒ to show what the tree looks like

   Ⓓ to show the people who damaged the tree

Informational Practice Exercise

A Woman Up a Tree (cont.)

Directions: Answer the questions.

7. How does this article make you feel? Tell the words that the author uses that cause this emotion.

_____

_____

_____

_____

8. Complete the Sum It Up chart using facts from the first two paragraphs of the article.

Sum It Up

Who	
Did What	
When	
Where	
Why	to protect Luna from being cut down

Name: _____ Date: _____

The Coral Reef Crisis

Directions: Read this text and respond to the questions on pages 31–33.

1 Under the clear blue sea, groups of ocean creatures live together in brightly colored structures. These underwater cities are called coral reefs. They have been around for millions of years.

2 But danger looms. Scientists are worried about the world's coral reefs. They have given a strong warning. Pollution and careless humans have wrecked more than a quarter of all reefs. If things don't improve soon, all the reefs may die in the next 20 years. That would put thousands of sea creatures at risk of dying out.

Precious Habitats

3 Coral seems like rock. It has a stone-like surface. But it is actually made up of tiny clear animals. They are coral polyps. Many are less than one inch wide. Millions of coral polyps stick together. They form colonies. They grow a hard shell. As these colonies grow bigger, they merge. They make big reefs. The bright color of coral comes from algae. Algae are tiny sea plants. Coral and algae depend on each other to live.

4 Coral may feel tough. Yet it's very delicate. Pollution has hurt many reefs. Bad fishing methods have also caused terrible harm. One problem is when people throw dynamite into the water. They do it to shock fish. It makes them easier to catch. But it blows up part of the reef.

5 The biggest threat is that oceans are getting warmer. Warm water causes coral to lose the algae that provide its food and color. This deadly process is called coral bleaching.

The Coral Reef Crisis *(cont.)*

It's Time to Help

6 Scientists think that the reefs can still be saved. People must outlaw bad practices and control pollution. "The world's attitude must change," says scientist Clive Wilkinson. Maybe it already has. A group called the United Nations Foundation said it would give $10 million to help save the reefs. The money will be used to study reefs and teach people how to help.

Pollution has caused sea plants to strangle the reef in the photo on the left. Warm water has bleached the reef on the right.

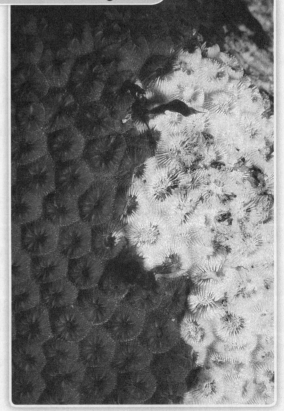

Bob Cranston/Mo Young Productions

Name: _____   Date: _____

The Coral Reef Crisis (cont.)

Directions: Fill in the bubble of each correct answer choice.

1. What might happen if ocean warming and pollution are not controlled?

   Ⓐ Underwater cities may be formed.

   Ⓑ There may be more pollution.

   Ⓒ Coral polyps may stick together.

   Ⓓ Most coral reefs may die in 20 years.

2. What is the author's purpose for writing this article?

   Ⓐ to inform readers about ocean pollution

   Ⓑ to teach readers about coral reefs

   Ⓒ to tell readers about the troubles coral reefs face

   Ⓓ to end fishing in the oceans

3. Which sentence from the article supports the answer for number 2?

   Ⓔ "Scientists are worried about the world's coral reefs."

   Ⓕ "One problem is when people throw dynamite into the water."

   Ⓖ "Coral seems like rock."

   Ⓗ "These underwater cities are called coral reefs."

Name: _____ Date: _____

The Coral Reef Crisis (cont.)

Directions: Fill in the bubble of each correct answer choice.

4. What is the biggest threat to coral reefs?

   Ⓐ Ocean water is getting warmer.

   Ⓑ People throw dynamite into the water.

   Ⓒ People pollute the oceans.

   Ⓓ Bad fishing methods are used.

5. What tone does the author communicate in the article?

   Ⓐ fear

   Ⓑ danger

   Ⓒ concern

   Ⓓ excitement

6. What is the main reason the author includes the photos at the end of the article?

   Ⓐ to show the dangers facing coral reefs

   Ⓑ to show great places to go snorkeling

   Ⓒ to provide more detail about coral colonies

   Ⓓ to add pretty images to the article

Name: _____ Date: _____

The Coral Reef Crisis *(cont.)*

Directions: Answer the questions.

7. Complete the graphic organizer with facts from the article about how coral reefs form.

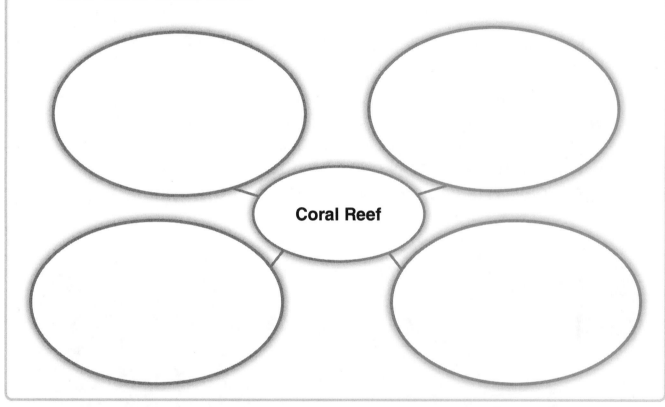

8. Write a sentence or two that summarizes your findings in the graphic organizer for number 7.

_____

_____

_____

_____

Name: _____   Date: _____

Undersea Volcanoes

Directions: Read this text and respond to the questions on pages 36–38.

1 No one has ever seen some of the world's biggest volcanoes. Why? They are deep under the sea. You would have to dive down a mile and a half just to reach the tops! This string of underwater volcanoes is called the Mid-Ocean Ridge.

2 The Mid-Ocean Ridge is the biggest mountain range on our planet. It's more than 30,000 miles long. It is almost 500 miles wide. It has hundreds of mountains and volcanoes. They zigzag under the sea between the continents. They wind their way around the globe like the seam on a baseball. Nearly every day, at least one underwater volcano erupts.

These volcanic islands formations rise right out of the water.

Undersea Volcanoes (cont.)

3 This means that the bottom of the sea is always changing. Hot lava comes from deep inside Earth. It pours out of the volcano. It spills onto the sea floor. As the lava cools, it forms rock. Layers of rocky lava pile up. Over millions of years, all that lava makes the sea floor expand. As the sea floor expands, it pushes the continents around. That is why a million years ago, the Earth looked very different than it does today. A million years from now, it will have changed again.

4 When volcanoes erupt underwater, they may form a mountain. This mountain may reach the surface of the sea. It forms a volcanic island. That's how Surtsey was created.

5 Surtsey first appeared in 1963. It is off the coast of Iceland. Iceland is an island nation. It is in the Atlantic Ocean. The erupting volcano had risen 300 feet from the bottom of the ocean. Icelanders named the new island after their god of fire.

6 For three and a half years, lava kept flowing. Surtsey grew and grew. At last the lava stopped in 1967. By then, the island was a mile wide and 560 feet high.

Woods Hole Oceanographic Institution

Each Hawaiian island began as an undersea volcano.

Name: _____ Date: _____

Undersea Volcanoes *(cont.)*

Directions: Fill in the bubble of each correct answer choice.

1. Which sentence from the article tells why people have not seen some of the the world's biggest volcanoes?

   Ⓐ "They are deep under the sea."

   Ⓑ "They wind their way around the globe like the seam on a baseball."

   Ⓒ "Hot lava comes from deep inside Earth."

   Ⓓ "It forms a volcanic island."

2. To what does the author compare the line of underwater volcanoes?

   Ⓐ a baseball

   Ⓑ the seam on a baseball

   Ⓒ layers of rocky lava

   Ⓓ the surface of the sea

3. What is the final stage in the formation of a volcanic island?

   Ⓐ Hot lava spills out and cools.

   Ⓑ A volcano erupts under water.

   Ⓒ Lava expands the floor of the sea.

   Ⓓ Lava builds up layers of rock.

Undersea Volcanoes *(cont.)*

Directions: Fill in the bubble of each correct answer choice.

4. What is the name of the largest mountain range on the planet?

   Ⓐ the Rocky Mountains

   Ⓑ the Iceland mountain range

   Ⓒ the Mid-Ocean Ridge

   Ⓓ the Undersea Volcano range

5. Which two sentences from the article support the answer to number 4?

   Ⓔ "It is almost 500 miles wide."

   Ⓕ "The erupting volcano had risen 300 feet from the bottom of the ocean."

   Ⓖ "It's more than 30,000 miles long."

   Ⓗ "You would have to dive down a mile and a half just to reach the tops!"

6. What can be inferred by the photo on page 35 and its caption?

   Ⓐ At one time, the Hawaiian islands did not exist.

   Ⓑ It would be dangerous to live on the Hawaiian islands.

   Ⓒ The Hawaiian islands are huge.

   Ⓓ The Hawaiian islands are far from the mainland of the United States.

Name: _____   Date: _____

Undersea Volcanoes (cont.)

Directions: Answer the questions.

7. Using information from the article, describe the Mid-Ocean Ridge.

_____

_____

_____

8. Complete the flow chart to describe how and when Surtsey formed.

Name: _____   Date: _____

She Gives Them Food for Thought

Directions: Read this text and respond to the questions on pages 40–42.

1   When it's time for science class, the kids at Martin Luther King Jr. Middle School start digging. They also start watering, weeding, and picking. Why? Their science class takes place in a garden.

2   The garden is in Berkeley, California. It is close to the students' school. It was started by a famous chef. Her name is Alice Waters. Waters helps the kids to grow carrots, strawberries, and other food. Everything in the garden is organic. That means it is grown without the use of harmful chemicals.

Thomas Heinser; bottom: Daniel Dobers

3   Waters runs a restaurant. She also wrote several cookbooks. She is known for using locally grown and organic foods. She started the garden so kids could learn about healthful eating. The students use the garden for more than science class. Math, art, and social studies lessons are also taught there.

4   Waters has a goal. She wants the kids to learn to prepare and eat healthful meals. Too many kids eat only fast food. Waters wants them to know what it's like to taste fresh, homegrown fruits and vegetables. It seems to be working.

5   "Every time I see the kids," Waters says, "I know the garden is a good idea."

Name: _____   Date: _____

She Gives Them Food for Thought (cont.)

Directions: Fill in the bubble of each correct answer choice.

1. What is unusual about the students' science class?

   Ⓐ It takes place at a restaurant.

   Ⓑ It takes place in a garden.

   Ⓒ It takes place in a classroom.

   Ⓓ They learn to eat healthy.

2. What does Alice Waters teach the students?

   Ⓐ how to run a restaurant

   Ⓑ how to do well in school

   Ⓒ how to grow food

   Ⓓ how to set goals

3. Which sentence supports the answer to number 2?

   Ⓔ "Waters helps the kids to grow carrots, strawberries, and other food."

   Ⓕ "Everything in the garden is organic."

   Ⓖ "She started the garden so kids could learn about healthful eating."

   Ⓗ "Waters runs a restaurant."

Name: _____   Date: _____

She Gives Them Food for Thought (cont.)

Directions: Fill in the bubble of each correct answer choice.

4. What message does the author want to communicate in the article?

- (A) Waters is a successful chef.
- (B) Waters likes children.
- (C) Waters likes to cook.
- (D) Waters is doing something new and different.

5. What fact can be inferred from the article?

- (A) Waters does not like to pull weeds.
- (B) Waters wants to be a school teacher.
- (C) Waters does not think chemicals should be used on food.
- (D) Waters is an unhealthy person.

6. The message communicated by the photographs is that . . .

- (A) science is the students' favorite class.
- (B) Waters is a cheerful person.
- (C) Waters enjoys growing food in the garden.
- (D) Waters works very hard as a chef.

Name: _____ Date: _____

She Gives Them Food for Thought *(cont.)*

Directions: Answer the questions.

7. What kinds of classes are taught using the garden? Use information from the article in your response.

_____

_____

_____

8. Complete the graphic organizer with things students learn by working in the garden.

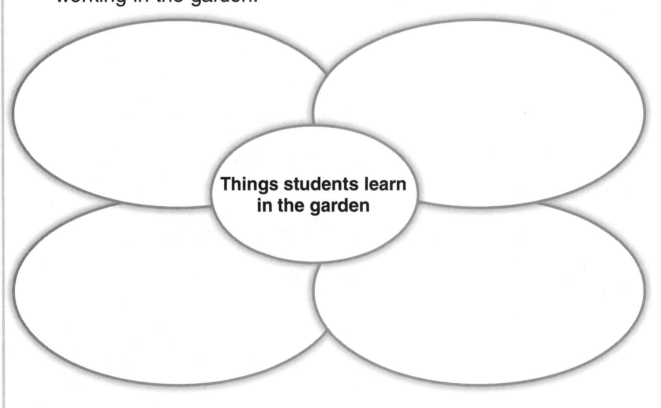

Things students learn in the garden

Name: _____   Date: _____

For Sale: Rare and Stolen Pets

Directions: Read this text and respond to the questions on pages 45–47.

1   Animals are jammed into cages at a market in Mexico City. Green parrots and toucans squawk loudly. Many of these animals are rare or endangered. That means there are very few left in the wild. Still, they are being snatched and sold as pets.

2   Cats and dogs have been pets for thousands of years. Wild animals do not make good pets. They bite. They wreck homes and belongings. Even with loving owners, they die from not having the right food or environment.

Gerry Ellis/ENP Images

A chimpanzee sits in a cage after an animal thief was caught in Rwanda, a country in Africa. The chimp will be returned to its forest home.

3 Despite the risks, people want to own wild animals. So, all over the world, rare birds, reptiles, and monkeys are stolen from the wild. They are sneaked into pet markets. This illegal trade is worth billions of dollars. Some people will pay lots of money for a rare pet. For example, a scarlet macaw is a bird from Brazil. It can sell for $3,000.

4 Often poor people steal rare animals from the wild. They do it because they have no other income. They sell the animals to smugglers. The animals are taken to countries such as the United States.

5 Since it is against the law, the smugglers have to sneak the animals into the country. Some hide live birds in tennis ball cans. Others tape lizards under their shirts or put them into big suitcases with false bottoms.

6 The United States works with other countries to stop this trade. But there's just one sure way to end it. People must stop buying wild animals.

7 Jorge Picon works for the U.S. Fish and Wildlife Service. He works to keep rare animals out of pet stores. "Every shipment I see breaks my heart," he says. "These animals belong in the wild."

For Sale: Rare and Stolen Pets *(cont.)*

Directions: Fill in the bubble of each correct answer choice.

1. What is a synonym for the word *snatched* as used in paragraph 1?

   Ⓐ abused

   Ⓑ adopted

   Ⓒ collected

   Ⓓ stolen

2. Which sentence from the article supports the answer to number 1?

   Ⓔ "Many of these animals are rare or endangered."

   Ⓕ "Wild animals do not make good pets."

   Ⓖ "Often poor people steal rare animals from the wild."

   Ⓗ "They sell the animals to smugglers."

3. Why is it against the law to sell rare pets?

   Ⓐ They destroy homes.

   Ⓑ They are endangered.

   Ⓒ They cost too much.

   Ⓓ They bite people.

Name: _____   Date: _____

For Sale: Rare and Stolen Pets (cont.)

Directions: Fill in the bubble of each correct answer choice.

4. What is the main message of the article?

- Ⓐ Poor people need another way to earn money.
- Ⓑ Macaws are almost extinct.
- Ⓒ Don't buy rare and endangered animals for pets.
- Ⓓ People should not own pets.

5. According to the article, what would be the effect if no one bought rare animals?

- Ⓐ They would no longer be stolen and smuggled.
- Ⓑ Pet stores would go out of business.
- Ⓒ Poor people would starve.
- Ⓓ The animals would die in the wild.

6. What can be inferred from the photograph and its caption?

- Ⓐ The chimp will be free.
- Ⓑ The chimp is going to be sold.
- Ⓒ The chimp will be taken far from home.
- Ⓓ The chimp will be owned as a pet.

For Sale: Rare and Stolen Pets (cont.)

Directions: Answer the questions.

7. Write a message to a friend telling why it is not good to buy a rare pet. Use three facts from the article.

   _____

   _____

   _____

   _____

8. Using the text, complete the graphic organizer.

What is the problem?	How can it be solved?
Who?	Why?
Where?	

Name: _____   Date: _____

Threads of Kindness

Directions: Read this text and respond to the questions on pages 49–51.

1   More than 30 years ago, Tran Duyen Hai went for a walk. Tran lives in Hanoi. It is the capital city of Vietnam. It is a country in Southeast Asia. Tran's walk that day took him around the shore of a large lake. He saw two teenage girls sitting by the path. They were crying.

2   "They looked so miserable," he says. "I went over to talk to them."

3   As he got nearer, he noticed both girls were disabled. They couldn't walk.

4   "They told me they'd been to a government job-training center but had been turned away."

Tran teaches disabled teenagers to sew.

Peter Charlesworth/On Asia Images

5   A lightbulb went on in Tran's mind. His job was training people to work in a garment factory. It was work that someone could do sitting down. He offered to give the girls free sewing lessons. They agreed. To Tran's surprise, seven disabled girls showed up for the first lesson. A month later, Tran had 12 students, then 25. He retired from his job. He wanted to spend all his time teaching disabled kids.

6   Ever since, Tran has run a center for disabled children. He started the center with $1,500 of his own savings. Now he gets help from his family and from charities. He has helped to find jobs for thousands of teenagers.

7   Do Thi Toan is one of Tran's former students. She used to worry about finding a good job. Today, she earns enough to send some money to her family. She and all his other students are very happy that Tran took that walk around the lake.

Name: _____   Date: _____

Threads of Kindness *(cont.)*

Directions: Fill in the bubble of each correct answer choice.

1. Reread paragraph 5. What is a *garment factory*?

   Ⓐ a company where clothes are made

   Ⓑ a company that teaches people how to sew

   Ⓒ a place that helps people who cannot walk

   Ⓓ a government training center

2. How does teaching the teenagers to sew help them?

   Ⓐ It gives them something to do.

   Ⓑ It makes them smile.

   Ⓒ They are able to get jobs.

   Ⓓ They make their own clothes.

3. Which sentence from the article supports the answer to number 2?

   Ⓔ "It was work that someone could do sitting down."

   Ⓕ "She used to worry about finding a good job."

   Ⓖ "They couldn't walk."

   Ⓗ "Now he gets help from his family and from charities."

Name: _____   Date: _____

Threads of Kindness (cont.)

Directions: Fill in the bubble of each correct answer choice.

---

4. Where does Tran go for a walk?

   Ⓐ near the garment factory

   Ⓑ around a lake

   Ⓒ near a school

   Ⓓ by a home for disabled girls

---

5. What is the author's main message?

   Ⓐ Sewing is fun.

   Ⓑ More people should learn how to sew.

   Ⓒ It is kind to talk to someone who is crying.

   Ⓓ It is wonderful to help people.

---

6. What does the reader learn from the photograph and caption?

   Ⓐ Tran teaches teenagers to sew in a classroom.

   Ⓑ Tran likes to make his own clothes.

   Ⓒ The girls make a lot of money.

   Ⓓ Tran is a nice man.

Name: _____ Date: _____

Threads of Kindness (cont.)

Directions: Answer the questions.

7. Based on evidence from the article, what words would you use to describe Tran?

   _____

   _____

   _____

   _____

8. List three problems that the girls faced before meeting Tran and how their problems were solved.

Problem Before Meeting Tran	How the Problem Was Solved
1.	1.
2.	2.
3.	3.

The Long Trail

from *The Call of the Wild* by Jack London

Directions: Read this story and respond to the questions on pages 53–55.

1 Buck was tired, more tired than he ever thought he could be. He and the other dogs had been on the trail for 30 days. They were hauling the sled from the town of Dawson to the town of Skagway in Alaska. That was more than 400 miles across the solidly frozen Yukon.

2 The Yukon was filled with optimistic men who had come to look for gold and seek their fortune. Most of them had wives or sweethearts back home. All of those loved ones wrote letters. So a pile of mail arrived by ship at Skagway. It had to be hauled by sled over the mountains to Dawson. Then all the answering letters had to be hauled back.

3 The wind was bitingly cold. The snow and ice hurt Buck's paws. It was even harder on the other dogs, who were smaller. The one called Sol-leks was limping and so was Pike. Dub's shoulder was aching painfully. All of them had aching paws.

4 There was no spring left in them; their feet fell heavily on the trail. There was nothing the matter with the dogs except that they were dead tired. Every muscle, every fiber, every cell was tired, dead tired.

5 "Mush on, poor sore feet!" the driver called. The men were tired, too. But that mountain of mail had to be delivered. The driver snapped his whip. "Mush on!" he shouted.

6 Buck lowered his head and strained against the harness. The sled moved on over the cold, stinging snow.

Name: _____   Date: _____

Literature Practice Exercise

The Long Trail (cont.)

Directions: Fill in the bubble of each correct answer choice.

1. Who or what is Buck?
   - Ⓐ a sled driver
   - Ⓑ a fortune seeker
   - Ⓒ a mailman
   - Ⓓ a dog

2. Which sentence supports the answer to number 1?
   - Ⓔ "Most of them had wives or sweethearts back home."
   - Ⓕ "The snow and ice hurt Buck's paws."
   - Ⓖ "'Mush on, poor sore feet!' the driver called."
   - Ⓗ "There was nothing the matter with the dogs except that they were dead tired."

3. What can the reader infer will happen next?
   - Ⓐ Buck will stop for a long rest.
   - Ⓑ Buck and the other dogs will keep going even though they are tired.
   - Ⓒ The sled driver will decide not to continue on.
   - Ⓓ The dogs will refuse to go any further.

© Shell Education   #51436—TIME For Kids: Practicing for Today's Tests   53

The Long Trail (cont.)

Directions: Fill in the bubble of each correct answer choice.

4. What does the word *optimistic* mean as used in paragraph 2?

   Ⓐ hard-working

   Ⓑ rich

   Ⓒ hopeful

   Ⓓ strong

5. What is one message that the author communicates?

   Ⓐ Surviving in the Yukon is not easy.

   Ⓑ It is hard for people to be separated from loved ones.

   Ⓒ There are lots of mountains in the Yukon.

   Ⓓ Sled dogs make good pets.

6. What is the best purpose of the illustration?

   Ⓐ to show how sled dogs work

   Ⓑ to show that sled dogs are beautiful

   Ⓒ to show how fun it is to ride a dog sled

   Ⓓ to show that Alaska is snowy

Name: _____   Date: _____

The Long Trail (cont.)

Directions: Answer the questions.

7. Imagine you are one of the sled dogs running with Buck. Using words from the story, write how you feel about pulling the sled.

_____

_____

_____

_____

_____

8. Complete the graphic organizer with words from the text that describe the dogs' conditions.

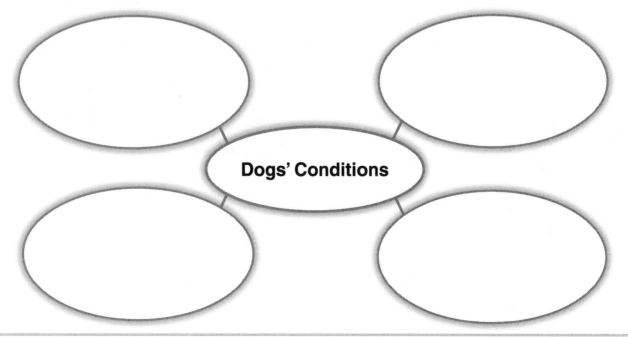

Dogs' Conditions

Name: _____   Date: _____

Paul Bunyan

Directions: Read this story and respond to the questions on pages 57–59.

1   Five storks delivered a huge baby to the Bunyans. They lived in Bangor, Maine. The parents named him Paul.

2   To fill Paul's bottle, the Bunyans milked 24 cows from sunrise to sunset. For breakfast, Paul ate 10 barrels of porridge.

3   Paul destroyed forests as he rolled around in his sleep. So his parents built a raft and let the napping baby float in the ocean. But Paul turned over and caused a tidal wave. The Bunyans realized the eastern United States was too small for Paul. They moved to Minnesota.

4   One day when he was a young man, Paul saw a tiny blue ox struggling to climb a snowdrift. Paul took the ox home and warmed him by the fire. Even once the ox warmed up, it remained blue. Paul decided to call him Babe the Blue Ox.

Matt Collins for Time For Kids

5   Babe grew to unreal proportions. It took a whole day for a bird to fly from one of his horns to the other! Babe ate 30 bales of hay just as a snack.

6   Babe helped Paul with his job as a lumberjack. They left their mark wherever they roamed. As they stomped around Minnesota, they made giant footprints in the ground. Rain filled their tracks. And that is how the state's famous 10,000 lakes were formed.

Paul Bunyan (cont.)

Directions: Fill in the bubble of each correct answer choice.

1. Which detail shows just how much Paul's parents are willing to do for him?

   Ⓐ They get him an ox.

   Ⓑ They move to Minnesota so he can have more space.

   Ⓒ They ask storks for a baby.

   Ⓓ They want him to be a lumberjack.

2. What is the Paul Bunyan story?

   Ⓐ a fable

   Ⓑ a mystery

   Ⓒ a nursery rhyme

   Ⓓ a folktale

3. How are Paul and Babe similar?

   Ⓐ They are both from Bangor, Maine.

   Ⓑ They are both very big.

   Ⓒ They both drink a lot of milk.

   Ⓓ They both move to Minnesota.

Name: _____ Date: _____

Paul Bunyan *(cont.)*

Directions: Fill in the bubble of each correct answer choice.

4. What does it mean that Babe grew to *unreal proportions*?

   Ⓐ Babe was very tiny.

   Ⓑ Babe causes a tidal wave when he walks.

   Ⓒ Babe eats a lot of food.

   Ⓓ Babe grows so large it is hard to imagine.

5. What sentence supports the answer to number 4?

   Ⓔ "Even once the ox warmed up, it remained blue."

   Ⓕ "Babe helped Paul with his job as a lumberjack."

   Ⓖ "It took a whole day for a bird to fly from one of his horns to the other!"

   Ⓗ "They left their mark wherever they roamed."

6. What is the best purpose of the illustration?

   Ⓐ to show that Paul's family lives in a log cabin

   Ⓑ to show that Babe is Paul's friend

   Ⓒ to show how much bigger Paul and Babe are compared to everything else

   Ⓓ to show that Paul likes being a lumberjack

Name: _____   Date: _____

Paul Bunyan (cont.)

Directions: Answer the questions.

7. Write three examples from the story that let the reader know that it is fictional.

_____

_____

_____

_____

8. Complete the Venn diagram to compare Baby Paul to a typical baby.

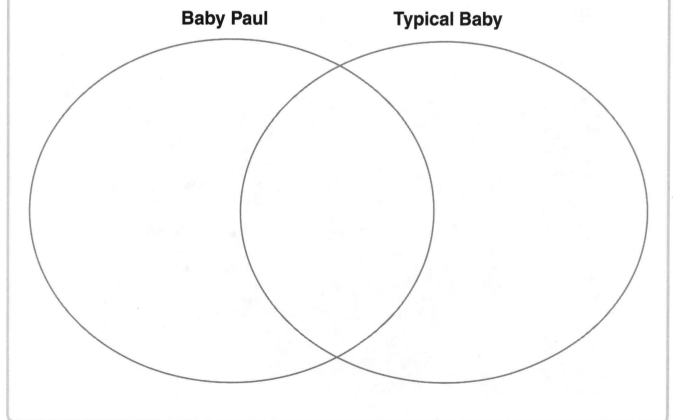

Baby Paul   **Typical Baby**

Name: _____   Date: _____

Go Fly a Kite!

Directions: Read this story and respond to the questions on pages 62–64.

1   I was just leaving my house when my mother called out to me. "Ezra, did you take your key with you?" My mother held out the key in her hand. I grabbed it, and she said sternly, "A ten-year-old boy must not be locked out of his house."

2   I had a good reason to forget my key. I was about to see Philadelphia's greatest citizen, Benjamin Franklin. Of course, Ben was not expecting me on this June day in 1752. Nor was his son, William. Neither one knew me, but I knew of them.

3   By accident, I had heard William tell a shopkeeper that he and his father were going to fly a kite this day. I knew he was up to something, and I wanted to watch the genius at work. I knew where Ben Franklin lived—everyone in Philadelphia did. So I waited outside his house. Soon, father and son left the house carrying some large objects.

David Wenzel

Go Fly a Kite! *(cont.)*

4 I followed them to a farm right outside the city and hid behind a tree. Ben and William watched the sky, and as storm clouds gathered, Ben said, "Let's get ready."

5 Ben attached a string to the kite. Then he looked around for something. "Where is the key, William?" he asked. His son looked in his pockets but found no key.

6 "I cannot do the experiment without a key," said Ben. "We might as well go home."

7 At that moment, I leaped from behind the tree. "Mr. Franklin, I have a key." I held up the key to my house.

8 I glowed with pride when Ben exclaimed, "You have saved the day, young man!" I handed him the key, and he tied it near the end of the string. Next, he attached a metal wire to the key, which led to a glass jar.

9 Ben said to me, "I am performing an experiment to see if lightning is made of electricity. If it is, the electricity will be drawn from the kite to the metal key. Then it will flow into this special jar that collects electricity."

10 William got the kite flying, as rain began to fall. Holding the kite string, Ben led us into a nearby barn to stay dry. Before long, we saw a flash of lightning. Did his experiment work? Ben put his hand near the key. An electric spark jumped from the key to his fingers.

11 "We have done it!" he exclaimed. "We proved that lightning is made of electricity. And I could not have done it without you," he said to me.

12 When I got home, I realized I had left my key with Ben. I had helped unlock a secret of nature—but I couldn't unlock my front door!

Name: _____   Date: _____

Go Fly a Kite! *(cont.)*

Directions: Fill in the bubble of each correct answer choice.

1. What does the phrase *unlock a secret of nature* from paragraph 12 mean?

   (A) use a key to open a door

   (B) discover something new about the world

   (C) fly a kite in a storm

   (D) keep a secret you have been told

2. How well-known is Ben Franklin in 1752?

   (A) He is not known by many people.

   (B) No one knows who he is.

   (C) The people who live nearby know him.

   (D) Everybody in the city knows him.

3. Which sentence from the text supports the answer to number 2?

   (E) "I knew he was up to something, and I wanted to watch the genius at work."

   (F) "I knew where Ben Franklin lived—everyone in Philadelphia did."

   (G) "So I waited outside his house."

   (H) "Before long, we saw a flash of lightning."

Name: _____   Date: _____

Go Fly a Kite! *(cont.)*

Directions: Fill in the bubble of each correct answer choice.

4. What is the climax of the story?

ⓐ "William got the kite flying, as rain began to fall."

ⓑ "Ben said to me, 'I am performing an experiment to see if lightning is made of electricity.'"

ⓒ "An electric spark jumped from the key to his fingers."

ⓓ "When I got home, I realized I had left my key with Ben."

5. What is the author's purpose in writing this story?

ⓔ to let people know that Ben had a son

ⓕ to show that Ben was a scientist

ⓖ to tell a famous story from a different point of view

ⓗ to let people know that Ben took risks

6. What does the reader learn from the illustration?

ⓐ how men and boys dressed at that time

ⓑ that they all ended up soaking wet

ⓒ how Ezra got in trouble for losing his key

ⓓ that Ben enjoyed flying kites daily

Name: _____   Date: _____

Go Fly a Kite! (cont.)

Directions: Answer the questions.

7. Describe how Ezra feels when he helps with the experiment and then how he feels when he gets home. Use quotes from the passage in your response.

_____

_____

_____

_____

8. Use evidence from the article to complete the chart.

How Does Ezra Feel About Ben Franklin?	How Do You Know?
1.	1.
2.	2.

Name: _____   Date: _____

A Bedouin Tale

Directions: Read this story and respond to the questions on pages 67–69.

1   Bedouins are nomads who live in the deserts of Arabia. A long time ago, there was a Bedouin leader named Abu Yusef. He was known for his courage and fairness. For many years, he helped keep peace in the region. He stopped the many tribes from fighting one another. Then, one day, Abu Yusef became very ill. His three sons, Yusef, Zaid, and Omar, argued about who should take charge if their father died.

2   "I am the eldest, and it's only fair that I should be in power," Yusef said to the men of the tribe. Omar, the youngest son, said that since he was his father's favorite, he would make the best leader. The middle brother, Zaid, shouted, "It's clear that I should be the one in charge."

Drew Willis for Time For Kids

3   Abu Yusef heard the fighting among his sons. He felt very upset. He called his children to his bedside. "My beloved sons, you must prove your strength to me," he said. "I want each of you to bring me the largest tree branch you can find." When they returned, Abu Yusef instructed each of them to break his branch.

4   "I can easily break this," said Yusef. And in one quick snap, it was broken. Abu Yusef then asked Zaid if he could do the same. Zaid broke an even larger branch. Omar did, too.

A Bedouin Tale *(cont.)*

5 But Abu Yusef did not look satisfied. He asked his sons to gather the broken branches and tie them all together. "Can one of you break all of these together?" he asked.

6 Each son took a turn. Each tried hard but without success.

7 "You see, my sons, each stick is easy to break on its own, but together, they are stronger. The same is true for you," Abu Yusef said.

8 The brothers understood their father's message: Alone, each son was weak, but together, they were strong.

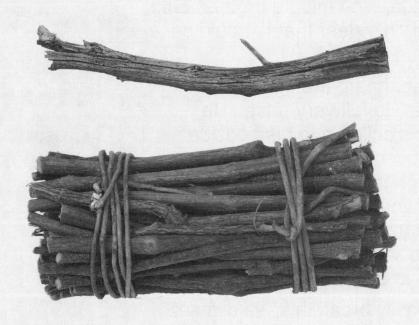

A Bedouin Tale (cont.)

Directions: Fill in the bubble of each correct answer choice.

1. What is the purpose of this story?

   Ⓐ to make people laugh

   Ⓑ to teach a lesson

   Ⓒ to entertain

   Ⓓ to provide factual information

2. What word best describes Abu Yusef?

   Ⓐ mean

   Ⓑ furious

   Ⓒ caring

   Ⓓ happy

3. Which sentence from the story supports the answer to number 2?

   Ⓔ "He stopped the many tribes from fighting one another."

   Ⓕ "Then, one day, Abu Yusef became very ill."

   Ⓖ "But Abu Yusef did not look satisfied."

   Ⓗ "Alone, each son was weak, but together, they were strong."

Name: _____   Date: _____

A Bedouin Tale *(cont.)*

Directions: Fill in the bubble of each correct answer choice.

4. Why is including the dialogue important to understanding the story? Choose all that apply.

   Ⓐ It helps the reader to understand that the sons are selfish.

   Ⓑ It helps the reader to understand that the father wants the sons to work together.

   Ⓒ It helps the reader to understand how the father works with other people.

   Ⓓ It helps the reader to understand Abu Yusef's life.

   Ⓔ It helps the reader understand that the father cares about his sons.

5. Which two sentences support the answer to number 4?

   Ⓕ "Each tried hard but without success."

   Ⓖ "His three sons, Yusef, Zaid, and Omar, argued about who should take charge if their father died."

   Ⓗ "You see, my sons, each stick is easy to break on its own, but together, they are stronger."

   Ⓘ "But Abu Yusef did not look satisfied."

6. What is the purpose of the illustration on page 65?

   Ⓐ to show how the men dressed

   Ⓑ to show that the father was unhappy with his sons

   Ⓒ to show how big the branches were

   Ⓓ to show how hard the brothers tried to prove their strength

A Bedouin Tale *(cont.)*

Name: _____   Date: _____

Directions: Answer the questions.

7. Explain how Abu Yusef's plan teaches his sons an important lesson. Use a quotation from the passage in your response.

_____

_____

_____

_____

_____

8. Based on information from the story, complete the graphic organizer with words that describe Abu Yusef.

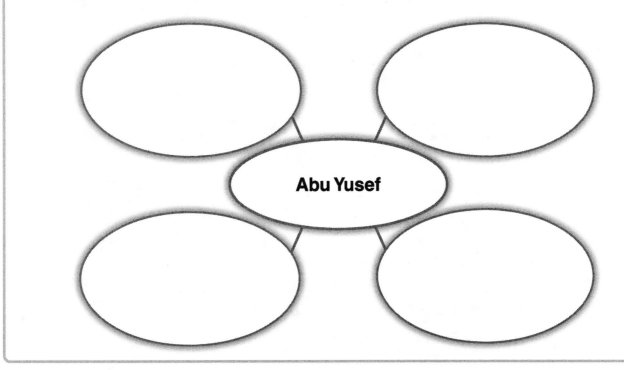

Name: _____   Date: _____

The Lion and the Wild Boar

Directions: Read this story and respond to the questions on pages 71–73.

1   One hot day a lion and a wild boar arrived at a pond at the same moment. "I got here first—wait your turn!" cried the wild boar. He blocked the lion's path.

2   "I am the king of all the beasts," roared the lion. "You should wait for me. I shouldn't have to drink water muddied by your hooves."

3   This angered the wild boar, and he attacked the lion, jabbing him with his sharp tusks. The lion grabbed the wild boar's throat with his teeth and would not let go. The brutal sun beat down on the thirsty pair until at last they both backed away from each other. Panting with exhaustion, they moved to opposite sides of the pond. While he rested, the lion looked up and noticed a group of buzzards clustered on a rock ledge, watching and waiting.

4   "Look up there," he said to the wild boar. "Those buzzards will eat whoever loses our battle. It doesn't matter to them whether it is me or you; they will pick clean the bones."

5   The wild boar looked at the birds. Then the lion and the wild boar looked at one another. "Let's stop fighting," they said at the same time.

6   The wild boar said, "Besides, there is plenty of water for us both." The lion added, "Drinking muddy water is better than being a buzzard's next meal."

7   Moral: Enemies will unite against a common enemy.

Name: _____   Date: _____

The Lion and the Wild Boar (cont.)

Directions: Fill in the bubble of each correct answer choice.

1. What will happen if the wild boar and the lion do not work out their differences?

   Ⓐ They will fight until one dies.

   Ⓑ They will go home.

   Ⓒ They will scare away the buzzards.

   Ⓓ They will make friends with the buzzards.

2. What is the story's main message?

   Ⓐ Fighting is bad.

   Ⓑ Lions and wild boars cannot be friends.

   Ⓒ Sometimes we have good reason to work with those we do not like.

   Ⓓ Sometimes animals can become friends.

3. Which sentence from the text supports the answer to number 2?

   Ⓔ "Enemies will unite against a common enemy."

   Ⓕ "The wild boar said, 'Besides, there is plenty of water for us both.'"

   Ⓖ "Drinking muddy water is better than being a buzzard's next meal."

   Ⓗ "It doesn't matter to them whether it is me or you; they will pick clean the bones."

The Lion and the Wild Boar (cont.)

Directions: Fill in the bubble of each correct answer choice.

Read this dictionary entry for the word *unite*.

unite (u-nite); verb

1. to join into a single unit
2. to stick together
3. to link in a legal bond
4. to combine by adhesion or mixture

4. Which meaning of *unite* is used in the last sentence?

- Ⓐ meaning 1
- Ⓑ meaning 2
- Ⓒ meaning 3
- Ⓓ meaning 4

5. Which sentence states the turning point in the story?

- Ⓐ "This angered the wild boar, and he attacked the lion, jabbing him with his sharp tusks."
- Ⓑ "Panting with exhaustion, they moved to opposite sides of the pond."
- Ⓒ "He blocked the lion's path."
- Ⓓ "Those buzzards will eat whoever loses our battle."

6. Why do the lion and wild boar modify their original stances? Choose all that apply.

- Ⓐ They change their opinions about each other.
- Ⓑ They know that they will die without water.
- Ⓒ They do not want to be eaten by the buzzards.
- Ⓓ They want to make friends with the buzzards.

Name: _____ Date: _____

The Lion and the Wild Boar (cont.)

Directions: Answer the questions.

7. At the start of the story, who has the better argument for drinking the water first, the lion or the wild boar?

_____

_____

_____

_____

8. Complete the Venn diagram to compare the lion and the wild boar.

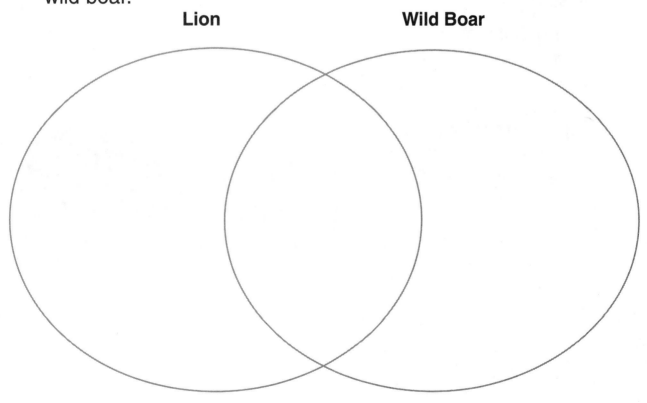

Lion   Wild Boar

© Shell Education   #51436—TIME For Kids: Practicing for Today's Tests   73

Name: _____ Date: _____

Racing a Tornado

Directions: Read this story and respond to the questions on pages 76–78.

1 If we had known what was going to happen, we never would have gotten on our bikes. But it seemed like a perfect day for a long bike ride. Maria and I set out at 7 A.M. and didn't stop for lunch until noon. We sat under an oak tree and had a picnic. That's when the sky began to change and we began to worry.

2 In the distance, a towering bank of dark clouds appeared. We looked at each other. There was no way we could avoid that storm. What could we do?

Corbis

The car sped away from the tornado as it came closer and closer.

Racing a Tornado (cont.)

3 The weather quickly got worse. The sky was very dark, not like daytime at all. Trees were bending in the wind. Suddenly, a blue car pulled up alongside our bikes. The woman at the wheel rolled down the side window and shouted, "Get in!" The driver looked as frightened as we felt. We abandoned our bikes in the ditch and jumped into the car just as colossal chunks of hail began to fall.

4 The car sped away, with hailstones the size of golf balls bouncing off the hood. Maria and I looked back at the black sky. Maria screamed and pointed, "There's a tornado!"

5 The black, twisting funnel seemed to be chasing us. It certainly was getting closer and closer. I was terrified. How could we outrun that monster?

6 "There's an overpass ahead," the driver said. "We'll use it for cover."

7 She brought the car to a stop under the bridge, and we all ran up the embankment. The woman yelled to us to lie flat. We squeezed down behind the concrete part of the structure, and not a minute too soon. A roaring like a freight train passed over us. Then, suddenly, it was over. We had survived—barely. That was a race we didn't ever want to run again!

Racing a Tornado (cont.)

Directions: Fill in the bubble of each correct answer choice.

1. What is the tone of the text?

   Ⓐ excitement

   Ⓑ joy

   Ⓒ fear

   Ⓓ anger

2. Which sentence best supports the answer to number 1?

   Ⓔ "Trees were bending in the wind."

   Ⓕ "The driver looked as frightened as we felt."

   Ⓖ "The woman yelled to us to lie flat."

   Ⓗ "How could we outrun that monster?"

3. What are the two purposes of the photo and caption?

   Ⓐ to show just how close the tornado was

   Ⓑ to show the size of the tornado

   Ⓒ to show the size of the hail

   Ⓓ to show the area where the kids live

Racing a Tornado *(cont.)*

Directions: Fill in the bubble of each correct answer choice.

4. What is the genre of this story?

- Ⓐ mystery
- Ⓑ fairy tale
- Ⓒ comedy
- Ⓓ suspense

5. Which is a synonym for the word *colossal* as used in paragraph 3?

- Ⓐ sharp
- Ⓑ cold
- Ⓒ huge
- Ⓓ interesting

6. Which two examples of dialogue best express the characters' feelings?

- Ⓐ "Maria screamed and pointed, 'There's a tornado!'"
- Ⓑ "The woman at the wheel rolled down the side window and shouted, 'Get in!'"
- Ⓒ "'There's an overpass ahead,' the driver said."
- Ⓓ "We'll use it for cover."

Name: _____ Date: _____

Racing a Tornado (cont.)

Directions: Answer the questions.

7. Use the text to describe why the narrator calls the tornado a monster.

   _____

   _____

   _____

   _____

8. Complete the graphic organizer to summarize what happens at the beginning, middle, and end of the story.

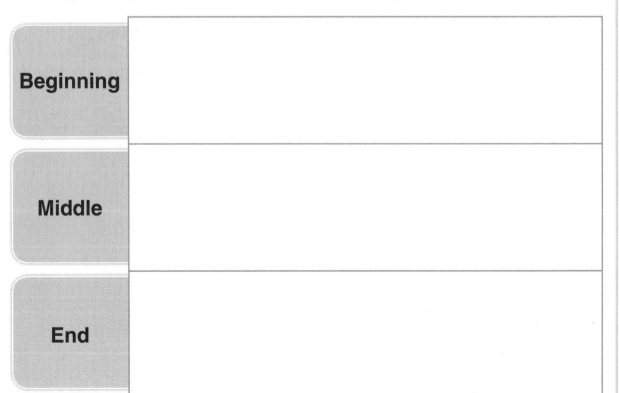

Name: _____   Date: _____

The Treasure Hunt

> **Directions:** Read this story and respond to the questions on pages 81–83.

1 Alex and Emma went walking on the beach. Emma pointed to something the tide had washed up on the shore.

2 Alex picked up the object. It was a glass bottle sealed tightly with a cork. There was something inside the bottle. Alex tried to pull out the cork, but it wouldn't budge. Emma grabbed it from him and managed to twist the cork out. She saw a paper in the bottle and pulled it out. She unfolded the paper. At the top were these words: "FOLLOW THE CLUES TO FIND A GREAT TREASURE!" Under this message was a set of clues.

3 Alex howled in excitement, "If we follow the clues, we'll find money or gold or diamonds!" They looked at the first number. The direction said: "It's where the money is."

4 "The place with money could be the bank," said Emma.

5 "Maybe," said Alex. He didn't like to admit his sister had good ideas. "Well, we can go there just in case."

6 Ten minutes later, they stood in front of the Sunshine Bank. There was lots of money inside, but it belonged to other people. There didn't seem to be any money hidden outside.

7 The clue for number two said, "Go two blocks north and one block west." The kids followed the directions and ended up at City Hall. They found nothing.

8 Clue three took them three blocks west to Paws Pet Store. Inside were sleepy kittens and puppies. A parrot squawked, "I dig it! I dig it!" The kids thought it might be a clue. "But dig where?" Alex asked the parrot. The parrot didn't answer. The store owner gave them a funny look.

9 The last clue said to go five blocks north and three blocks east. The pair ran the rest of the way. Gasping for breath, they stopped in front of the public library.

10 "What?" exclaimed Alex, disappointed. "There's no treasure here—just a lot of books."

11 "Let's go inside anyway," said Emma.

12 In the main room, the two looked at the clues again. What did *423.1 ref.* mean?

13 Emma walked up to the librarian and asked if she knew what it meant.

14 The librarian smiled and said, "Yes. It is a number in the Dewey Decimal System. Each nonfiction book has a Dewey Decimal number on its spine based on what type of book it is. That lets people easily find it on the shelves. The books are kept in numerical order. So go to the reference section and look until you find that number on the book's spine."

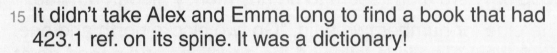

David Coulson

15 It didn't take Alex and Emma long to find a book that had 423.1 ref. on its spine. It was a dictionary!

16 "I don't get it!" said Alex unhappily. "This isn't a treasure. It's just an old book!"

17 Emma was silent for a moment. Then she said, "All the words in a language are in a dictionary. It helps us read, write, and speak. Without words, we couldn't say what we think and feel. We couldn't create ideas. Words let us move forward together. Look at how much we used words in this treasure hunt. This is a treasure after all!"

Name: _____ Date: _____

The Treasure Hunt *(cont.)*

Directions: Fill in the bubble of each correct answer choice.

1. Which two words best describe Emma?

   Ⓐ disappointed

   Ⓑ hopeful

   Ⓒ careless

   Ⓓ smart

2. How does Alex feel when they reach the library?

   Ⓐ disappointed

   Ⓑ excited

   Ⓒ nervous

   Ⓓ confused

3. Which sentence from the text supports the answer to number 2?

   Ⓔ "Clue three took them three blocks west to Paws Pet Store."

   Ⓕ "FOLLOW THE CLUES TO FIND A GREAT TREASURE!"

   Ⓖ "I dig it! I dig it!"

   Ⓗ "There's no treasure here—just a lot of books."

Name: _____   Date: _____

The Treasure Hunt (cont.)

Directions: Fill in the bubble of each correct answer choice.

4. At which point in the story are Alex and Emma most confused?

   Ⓐ when they find the bottle

   Ⓑ when they talk to the parrot

   Ⓒ when they are at the library

   Ⓓ when they discover that words are a treasure

5. What is one message the author communicates?

   Ⓐ There are different kinds of treasures.

   Ⓑ Looking for treasure is fun.

   Ⓒ People should work together.

   Ⓓ Librarians are helpful.

6. What is the purpose of the illustration?

   Ⓐ to show that the library is very large

   Ⓑ to show that Alex is upset to get a book as a treasure

   Ⓒ to show that they tell the librarian that they found the treasure

   Ⓓ to show the number of clues the children follow

The Treasure Hunt (cont.)

Directions: Answer the questions.

7. Explain how words in a dictionary are a treasure. Use at least one quotation from the text in your response.

    _____

    _____

    _____

8. Complete the flow chart to show where Alex and Emma go as they follow the clues in order.

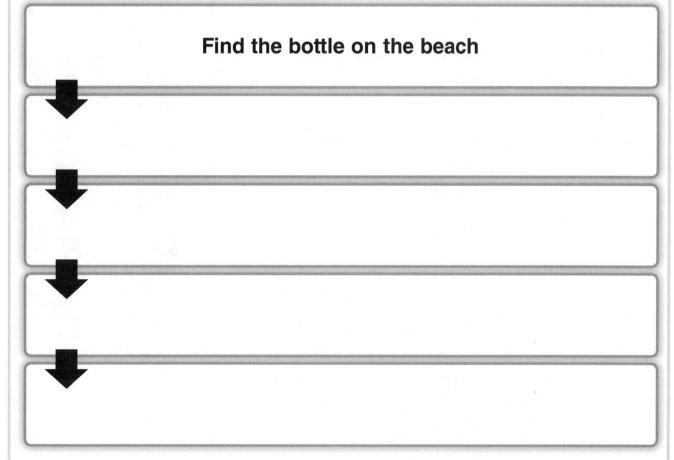

Find the bottle on the beach

Name: _____   Date: _____

It's a Dog's Life

Directions: Read this story and respond to the questions on pages 86–88.

1   "C'mon Butch, get the ball." Andy threw the ball and Butch raced across the yard. The dog caught the ball in his mouth, ran back to Andy, and dropped it at his feet. Ten minutes later, Andy said, "I know you love this game, but it's time to stop." Butch looked like he was smiling.

2   "I wish I knew what you're thinking, Butch," said Andy.

3   The next morning, Andy felt something wet. It was Butch licking his face. Suddenly, Andy heard, "I have to go out. Hurry up!"

4   Andy looked around but only Butch was in the room.

5   "Andy is so lazy."

6   Andy sat up in bed. "Who said that?"

7   "I'll try licking him again."

8   As Butch began to lick Andy, Andy jumped back. He thought, *I'm hearing things in my head, but there's no one around… except Butch.* "If I don't go outside right away, there's going to be an accident inside."

9   Andy was hearing Butch's thoughts! "Can you understand me?" Andy said aloud.

10 "Does he think I can talk?" Andy heard Butch think.

11 Andy was shocked and excited. Who could he tell about this? People would think he was nuts. "So, uh, Butch, you want to go outside?" asked Andy.

It's a Dog's Life (cont.)

12 "I thought you'd never ask," thought Butch.

13 Outside, Andy picked up a ball and tossed it. "Fetch it, Butch!"

14 "Doesn't he ever get tired of this game? I know I do."

15 Andy was surprised; he'd been certain that Butch loved this game.

16 "Let's go for a walk, Butch." Andy put a leash on Butch. At the dog park, Andy unhooked the leash to let Butch play with other dogs. In the distance, he could pick up some of Butch's thoughts: "Andy is okay for a human," he told one of the other pooches.

17 "And I thought he really loved me," Andy thought, feeling a bit discouraged.

18 Later, at dinner, Andy put out a bowl of dog food. "Hey, Butch! Come and get it."

19 "Same old stuff, day after day. I want human food."

20 Andy and his family were eating at the kitchen table. He heard Butch think, "I smell steak—that's my favorite!" A second later, Butch was sitting next to Andy, staring at the steaks.

21 "No, Butch!" yelled Andy's mother. "Get down!"

22 "They won't even give me a taste? They're so selfish." Butch jumped up on the table, grabbed a steak, and ran out of the dining room.

23 Andy found Butch, curled up in his favorite spot. He stopped to hear his dog's thoughts:

24 "I play with them, walk with them, let them pet me, guard their house. And then they get upset over a piece of meat. It's not easy being a dog."

It's a Dog's Life (cont.)

Directions: Fill in the bubble of each correct answer choice.

1. Which two things about Butch surprise Andy?

   Ⓐ He thinks Butch really loves him.

   Ⓑ He can hear Butch's thoughts.

   Ⓒ He finds out that Butch wants to eat steak.

   Ⓓ He learns that Butch wants to go for a walk.

2. How does Butch feel about playing fetch?

   Ⓐ He wants to play it all day.

   Ⓑ He would rather play fetch with other dogs.

   Ⓒ It is his favorite game.

   Ⓓ He only wants to play for a short time.

3. Which quotation from the story supports the answer to number 2?

   Ⓔ "'So, uh, Butch, you want to go outside?' asked Andy."

   Ⓕ "Doesn't he ever get tired of this game? I know I do."

   Ⓖ "Fetch it, Butch!"

   Ⓗ "At the dog park, Andy unhooked the leash to let Butch play with other dogs."

It's a Dog's Life (cont.)

Directions: Fill in the bubble of each correct answer choice.

4. In the story, what is the meaning of the word *nuts* as used in paragraph 11?

   Ⓐ happy

   Ⓑ discouraged

   Ⓒ hard-shelled, dry seeds

   Ⓓ crazy

5. What is the author's purpose for writing this story?

   Ⓐ to show that dogs do not like people

   Ⓑ to show that people are selfish

   Ⓒ to show that dogs do not always think what we expect

   Ⓓ to show that dogs really like boys

6. What is the purpose of the picture?

   Ⓐ to illustrate the friendship between the boy and his dog

   Ⓑ to show that Butch loves to play fetch

   Ⓒ to illustrate part of the action in the story

   Ⓓ to show that dogs like to play in parks

Name: _____   Date: _____

It's a Dog's Life (cont.)

Directions: Answer the questions.

7. Number the events of the story in the order in which they occur.

   _____ Andy can hear Butch's thoughts.

   _____ Andy feels Butch lick his face.

   _____ Butch is upset that he cannot have human food.

   _____ Andy takes Butch to the park.

   _____ Butch talks to dogs at the park.

8. Explain the emotions Andy feels using words from the text.

   _____

   _____

   _____

   _____

   _____

   _____

   _____

   _____

Name: _____   Date: _____

Windy Nights

by Robert Louis Stevenson

Directions: Read this poem and respond to the questions on pages 90–92.

1   Whenever the moon and stars are set,
      Whenever the wind is high,
    All night long in the dark and wet,
      A man goes riding by.
    Late in the night when the fires are out,
    Why does he gallop and gallop about?

7   Whenever the trees are crying aloud,
      And ships are tossed at sea,
    By, on the highway, low and loud,
      By at the gallop goes he.
    By at the gallop he goes, and then
    By he comes back at the gallop again.

Windy Nights (cont.)

Directions: Fill in the bubble of each correct answer choice.

1. Read lines 3–4 from the poem: "All night long in the dark and wet, A man goes riding by." What does the man represent?

   Ⓐ a horseback rider

   Ⓑ the rain

   Ⓒ the movement of air

   Ⓓ the trees

2. The author uses figurative language about. . .

   Ⓐ the moon and stars

   Ⓑ trees

   Ⓒ fires

   Ⓓ ships

3. Which line from the poem supports the answer to number 2?

   Ⓔ "Whenever the moon and stars are set"

   Ⓕ "Late in the night when the fires are out"

   Ⓖ "And ships are tossed at sea"

   Ⓗ "Whenever the trees are crying aloud"

Windy Nights *(cont.)*

Directions: Fill in the bubble of each correct answer choice.

4. How does the man move on his horse in the poem?

  Ⓐ very quietly

  Ⓑ back and forth

  Ⓒ in the daytime

  Ⓓ with a high scream

5. Which word in the poem best helps you to visualize the man's movement through the town?

  Ⓐ gallop

  Ⓑ loud

  Ⓒ moon

  Ⓓ highway

6. The whole poem is a metaphor for. . .

  Ⓐ a foggy night

  Ⓑ a storm

  Ⓒ a horseback rider

  Ⓓ the wind

Name: _____ Date: _____

Windy Nights (cont.)

Directions: Answer the questions.

7. Use phrases from the poem to explain how the author describes the title.

   _____

   _____

   _____

   _____

8. This poem uses a rhyming pattern. Complete the word web with four pairs of rhyming words from the poem.

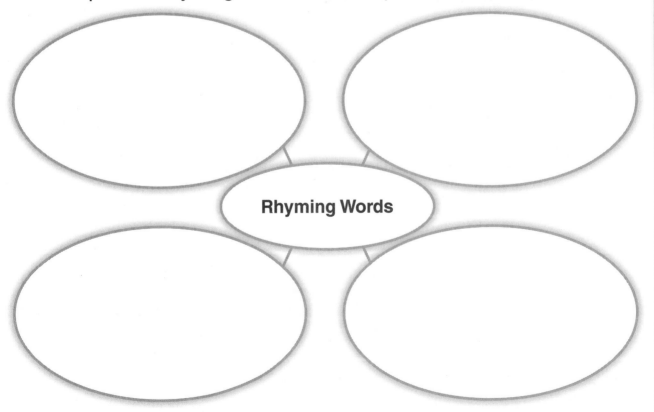

Name: _____   Date: _____

A Pleasant Day

by Eliza Lee Cabot Follen

Directions: Read this poem and respond to the questions on pages 94–96.

1   Come, my children, come away,
    For the sun shines bright today;
    Little children, come with me,
    Birds and brooks and flowers see;
    Get your hats and come away,
    For it is a pleasant day.

7   Everything is laughing, singing,
    All the pretty flowers are springing;
    See the kittens, full of fun,
    Tumbling in the brilliant sun;
    Children, too, may skip and play,
    For it is a pleasant day.

13 Bring the hoop and bring the ball,
    Come with happy faces all;
    Let us make a merry ring,
    Talk and laugh and dance and sing.
    Quickly, quickly, come away,
    For it is a pleasant day.

Name: _____ Date: _____

A Pleasant Day (cont.)

Directions: Fill in the bubble of each correct answer choice.

1. What makes the author believe that it is a pleasant day?

    Ⓐ "Children, too, may skip and play"

    Ⓑ "Get your hats and come away"

    Ⓒ "For the sun shines bright today"

    Ⓓ "Let us make a merry ring"

2. What feeling does the author convey to the reader?

    Ⓐ happiness

    Ⓑ sadness

    Ⓒ fear

    Ⓓ anger

3. Which line from the poem supports the answer to number 2?

    Ⓔ "For the sun shines bright today"

    Ⓕ "Birds and brooks and flowers see"

    Ⓖ "Everything is laughing, singing"

    Ⓗ "Quickly, quickly, come away"

Name: _____ Date: _____

A Pleasant Day (cont.)

Directions: Fill in the bubble of each correct answer choice.

4. Which word is the best synonym for *pleasant*?

   Ⓐ nice

   Ⓑ hopeful

   Ⓒ perfect

   Ⓓ cloudy

5. What does the author want the children to notice? There is more than one right answer.

   Ⓐ "See the kittens, full of fun"

   Ⓑ "Talk and laugh and dance and sing"

   Ⓒ "Birds and brooks and flowers see"

   Ⓓ "All the pretty flowers are springing"

   Ⓔ "Bring the hoop and bring the ball"

   Ⓕ "Come with happy faces all"

6. Which line from the poem expresses an opinion?

   Ⓐ "Children, too, may skip and play"

   Ⓑ "Get your hats and come away"

   Ⓒ "Bring the hoop and bring the ball"

   Ⓓ "For it is a pleasant day"

Name: _____ Date: _____

A Pleasant Day *(cont.)*

Directions: Answer the questions.

7. How does this poem make you feel? Tell the words that the author uses that cause this emotion.

_____

_____

_____

_____

8. Complete the web with words from the poem that describe three things that the children will hear on the pleasant day.

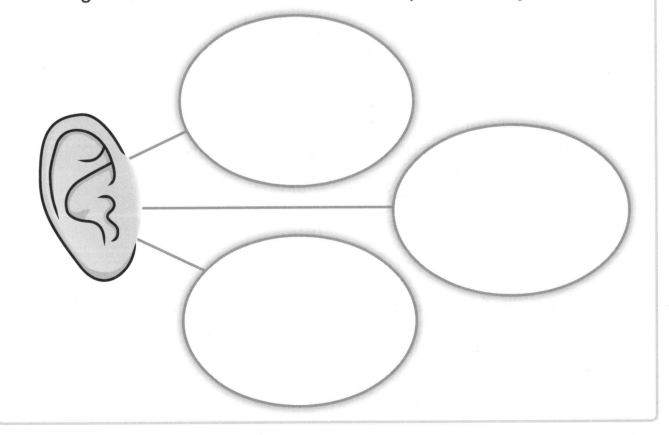

Name: _____   Date: _____

The Plumpuppets

by Christopher Morley

Directions: Read this poem and respond to the questions on pages 98–100.

1 When little heads weary have gone to their bed,
   When all the good nights and the prayers have been said,
   Of all the good fairies that send babes to rest
   The little Plumpuppets are those I love best.

5 If your pillow is lumpy, or hot, thin, and flat,
   The little Plumpuppets know just what they're at.
   They plump up the pillow, all soft, cool, and fat.
   The little Plumpuppets plump up it!

9 The little Plumpuppets are fairies of beds.
   They have nothing to do but to watch sleepyheads.
   They turn down the sheets, and they tuck you in tight.
   And then dance on your pillow to wish you good night!

Name: _____   Date: _____

The Plumpuppets (cont.)

Directions: Fill in the bubble of each correct answer choice.

1. What is a *Plumpuppet*?

   Ⓐ a fairy

   Ⓑ a puppet

   Ⓒ a sleeping child

   Ⓓ a pillow

2. What is the job of a *Plumpuppet*?

   Ⓐ to wave wands that make children fall asleep

   Ⓑ to sing lullabies to children

   Ⓒ to make children comfortable so they fall asleep

   Ⓓ to leave money under children's pillows

3. Which line from the poem supports the answer to number 2?

   Ⓔ "The little Plumpuppets are fairies of beds."

   Ⓕ "They plump up the pillow, all soft, cool, and fat."

   Ⓖ "And then dance on your pillow to wish you good night!"

   Ⓗ "When little heads weary have gone to their bed,"

The Plumpuppets (cont.)

Directions: Fill in the bubble of each correct answer choice.

Read this dictionary entry for the word *weary.*

weary \weer-ee\; adjective

1. bored
2. annoyed
3. tired
4. impatient

4. Which meaning of *weary* is used in the first line of the poem?

(A) meaning 1

(B) meaning 2

(C) meaning 3

(D) meaning 4

5. What does the author mean by the phrase "plump up it"?

(A) making a mattress softer

(B) turning down bed sheets

(C) jumping on a bed

(D) fluffing up a pillow

6. Which line of the poem expresses the author's opinion about Plumpuppets?

(A) "The little Plumpuppets know just what they're at."

(B) "The little Plumpuppets are those I love best."

(C) "The little Plumpuppets plump up it!"

(D) "They have nothing to do but to watch sleepyheads."

The Plumpuppets (cont.)

Directions: Answer the questions.

7. Why are the fairies called Plumpuppets? Support your answer with information from the poem.

_____

_____

_____

8. Using the text, complete the graphic organizer.

What Plumpuppets Do

Name: _____ Date: _____

Mr. Macklin's Jack O'Lantern
by David McCord

Directions: Read this poem and respond to the questions on pages 102–104.

1 Mr. Macklin takes his knife
   And carves the yellow pumpkin face:
   Three holes bring eyes and nose to life;
   The mouth has thirteen teeth in place.

5 Then Mr. Macklin, just for fun,
   Transfers the corn cob pipe from his
   Wry mouth to Jack's, and everyone
   Dies laughing! O what fun it is!

9 Till Mr. Macklin draws the shade
   And lights the candle in Jack's skull
   Then all the inside dark is made
   As spooky and as horrorful

13 As Halloween, and creepy crawl
   The shadows on the tool-house floor.
   With Jack's face dancing on the wall.
   Oh, Mr. Macklin! Where's the door?

Name: _____   Date: _____

Mr. Macklin's Jack O'Lantern (cont.)

Directions: Fill in the bubble of each correct answer choice.

1. Which two emotions does the poem communicate?

 Ⓐ excitement and joy

 Ⓑ anger and fear

 Ⓒ joy and fright

 Ⓓ happiness and anger

2. What is another term for *draws the shade* as used in line 9?

 Ⓐ pulls down the blind

 Ⓑ draws a dark picture

 Ⓒ turns off the lights

 Ⓓ lights a candle

3. What does everyone do when Mr. Macklin puts a pipe in the pumpkin's mouth?

 Ⓐ They scream.

 Ⓑ They run away.

 Ⓒ They hide.

 Ⓓ They laugh.

Poetry Practice Exercise

#51436—TIME For Kids: Practicing for Today's Tests

© Shell Education

102

Name: _____   Date: _____

Mr. Macklin's Jack O'Lantern (cont.)

Directions: Fill in the bubble of each correct answer choice.

4. What action occurs that changes the mood in the poem?

   Ⓐ The room gets dark and Mr. Macklin lights a candle.

   Ⓑ Mr. Macklin puts the Jack O'Lantern in the window.

   Ⓒ Mr. Macklin puts a pipe in Jack's mouth.

   Ⓓ Mr. Macklin carves the pumpkin.

5. Which line from the poem supports the answer to number 4?

   Ⓔ "Three holes bring eyes and nose to life;"

   Ⓕ "Mr. Macklin takes his knife"

   Ⓖ "Then all the inside dark is made as spooky and as horrorful"

   Ⓗ "The shadows on the tool-house floor"

6. What is the purpose of the illustration?

   Ⓐ to show that people feel afraid

   Ⓑ to show that Halloween is fun

   Ⓒ to teach the reader how to carve a pumpkin

   Ⓓ to show what Jack looks like

Name: _____   Date: _____

Mr. Macklin's Jack O'Lantern (cont.)

Directions: Answer the questions.

7. Number the steps in the order that Mr. Macklin does them to make his jack o'lantern.

_____ He lights a candle inside the pumpkin.

_____ He carves eyes and a nose.

_____ He puts his pipe into the pumpkin's mouth.

_____ He gets a knife.

_____ He carves thirteen teeth.

8. Who asks Mr. Macklin, "Where's the door?" Use a quotation from the poem in your response.

_____

_____

_____

_____

_____

_____

References Cited

Conley, David T. 2014. "Common Core Development and Substance." *Social Policy Report* 28 (2): 1–15.

Kornhaber, Mindy L., Kelly Griffith, and Alison Tyler. 2014. "It's Not Education by Zip Code Anymore—But What is It? Conceptions of Equity under the Common Core." *Education Policy Analysis Archives* 22 (4): 1–26. doi:10.14507/epaa.v22n4.2014.

National Governors Association Center for Best Practices, Council of Chief State School Officers. 2010. *Common Core State Standards*. National Governors Association Center for Best Practices, Council of Chief State School Officers: Washington D.C. http://www.corestandards.org/about-the-standards/frequently-asked-questions/.

Partnership for Assessment of Readiness for College and Careers. 2013. *The PARCC Assessment.* PARCC: Washington, D.C. http://www.parcconline.org/about-parcc.

Rothman, Robert. 2013. *Common Core State Standards 101*. http://all4ed.org/reports-factsheets/common-core-state-standards-101/.

Texas Education Agency. 2014. *State of Texas Assessment of Academic Readiness: A Parent's Guide to the Student Testing Program.* TEA: Texas.

The Smarter Balanced Assessment Consortium. 2014. *Smarter Balanced Assessment Consortium.* California Department of Education. http://www.smarterbalanced.org/about/member-states/.

Wiley, Terrence G., and Wayne E. Wright. 2004. "Against the Undertow: Language-Minority Education Policy and Politics in the 'Age of Accountability.'" *Educational Policy*, 18 (1): 142–168. doi:10.1177/0895904803260030.

Question Types

The following chart correlates each question in this book to one of the three categories of questions. For more information on the categories of questions, see pages 7–9.

Practice Exercise Title	Item	Key Ideas and Details	Craft and Structure	Integration of Knowledge and Ideas
Bats on the Brink (pages 13–17)	1	x		
	2	x		
	3	x		
	4		x	
	5		x	
	6			x
	7	x		
	8	x		
The Scoop on Sugar (pages 18–23)	1	x		
	2	x		
	3	x		
	4		x	
	5		x	
	6			x
	7		x	
	8	x		
A Woman Up a Tree (pages 24–28)	1	x		
	2	x		
	3	x		
	4		x	
	5		x	
	6			x
	7		x	
	8	x		
The Coral Reef Crisis (pages 29–33)	1	x		
	2		x	
	3	x		
	4	x		
	5		x	
	6			x
	7	x		
	8	x		
Undersea Volcanoes (pages 34–38)	1		x	
	2		x	
	3	x		
	4	x		
	5	x		
	6			x
	7	x		
	8	x		

Question Types *(cont.)*

Practice Exercise Title	Item	Key Ideas and Details	Craft and Structure	Integration of Knowledge and Ideas
She Gives Them Food for Thought (pages 39–42)	1	x		
	2	x		
	3	x		
	4		x	
	5		x	
	6			x
	7	x		
	8	x		
For Sale: Rare and Stolen Pets (pages 43–47)	1		x	
	2		x	
	3	x		
	4	x		
	5	x		
	6			x
	7	x		
	8	x		
Threads of Kindess (pages 48–51)	1		x	
	2	x		
	3	x		
	4	x		
	5		x	
	6			x
	7		x	
	8	x		
The Long Trail (pages 52–55)	1	x		
	2	x		
	3	x		
	4		x	
	5		x	
	6			x
	7		x	
	8	x		
Paul Bunyan (pages 56–59)	1	x		
	2		x	
	3	x		
	4		x	
	5	x		
	6			x
	7		x	
	8	x		

Question Types *(cont.)*

Practice Exercise Title	Item	Key Ideas and Details	Craft and Structure	Integration of Knowledge and Ideas
Go Fly a Kite! (pages 60–64)	1		x	
	2	x		
	3	x		
	4	x		
	5		x	
	6			x
	7	x		
	8		x	
A Bedouin Tale (pages 65–69)	1	x		
	2		x	
	3	x		
	4		x	
	5		x	
	6			x
	7		x	
	8	x		
The Lion and the Wild Boar (pages 70–73)	1	x		
	2	x		
	3	x		
	4		x	
	5		x	
	6			x
	7			x
	8	x		
Racing a Tornado (pages 74–78)	1		x	
	2		x	
	3			x
	4	x		
	5		x	
	6	x		
	7		x	
	8	x		
The Treasure Hunt (pages 79–83)	1	x		
	2	x		
	3	x		
	4		x	
	5		x	
	6			x
	7	x		
	8	x		

Question Types (cont.)

Practice Exercise Title	Item	Key Ideas and Details	Craft and Structure	Integration of Knowledge and Ideas
It's a Dog's Life (pages 84–88)	1	x		
	2	x		
	3	x		
	4		x	
	5		x	
	6			x
	7	x		
	8			x
Windy Nights (pages 89–92)	1		x	
	2		x	
	3	x		
	4	x		
	5			x
	6		x	
	7	x		
	8		x	
A Pleasant Day (pages 93–96)	1	x		
	2		x	
	3	x		
	4		x	
	5	x		
	6			x
	7		x	
	8	x		
The Plumpuppets (pages 97–100)	1	x		
	2	x		
	3	x		
	4		x	
	5		x	
	6			x
	7		x	
	8	x		
Mr. Macklin's Jack O'Lantern (pages 101–104)	1		x	
	2		x	
	3	x		
	4	x		
	5	x		
	6			x
	7	x		
	8		x	

Testing Tips

Reading

READ more nonfiction texts with students!

Writing

Encourage students to **SHOW** what they know with text-based **PROOF**!

How Do I Help Students Prepare for Today's Tests?

Mathematics

Help students **EXPLAIN** what's in their brains and **CONNECT** mathematics to the real world!

Listening

DISCUSS what you read! **ANALYZE** what you think! **SYNTHESIZE** information!!

Testing Tips *(cont.)*

Jail the Detail!		Highlight, underline, or circle the details in the questions. This helps FOCUS on what the question is asking.
Be Slick and Predict!		Predict what the answer is BEFORE you read the choices!
Slash the Trash!		Read ALL the answer choices. "Trash" the choices that you know are incorrect.
Plug It In! Plug It In!		Once you choose an answer, PLUG IT IN! Make sure your answer makes sense, especially with vocabulary and math.
Be Smart with Charts! Zap the Maps!		Charts and maps provide information that you can use to answer some questions. Analyze ALL information before answering a question!
Extra! Extra! Read All About It!		If the directions say read . . . READ! Pay close attention to signal words in the directions, such as *explain*, *interpret*, and *compare*.
If You Snooze, You Might Lose!		Do not leave questions unanswered. Answering questions increases your chances of getting correct answers!
Check It Out!		After you complete the test, go back and check your work!

Answer Key

Bats on the Brink (pages 13–17)

1. C. They are getting a fungus that makes them ill.

2. G. "A mysterious disease is killing bats."

3. D. the bats that hibernate

4. D. "People may not know it, but bats are helpful."

5. D. a person who works to protect animals and the environment

6. A. to give more details about bats

7. Possible answers include:

List two ways that bats are like people.	List three ways that bats are different from people.
1. drink milk	1. can fly
2. have hair	2. use echolocation
	3. eat mosquitoes

8. Bats eat mosquitoes. They also eat insects that carry disease and harm crops.

The Scoop on Sugar (pages 18–23)

1. A. Eat a balance of healthy foods and sugary foods.

2. H. "Replace some of those sugary foods with others that don't have added sugar."

3. C. 20 teaspoons

4. A. Eating too much sugar is bad for us.

5. B. a person who knows which foods are good and bad for us

6. D. to show who is eating sugar at various ages

7. I can change my diet to reduce the amount of sugar I eat by drinking fewer sodas, reading food labels, eating food with less sugar instead of sugary foods, eating foods with no added sugar, trying healthy new foods, eating more fruits and vegetables, eating fewer foods with sucrose, fructose, and syrup.

8.

Foods That Contain Too Much Sugar	Foods That Are Better For You
candy	fresh fruits
soda	vegetables
sugary cereal	meat
some pasta sauces, ketchup, crackers	
ice cream toppings	
processed foods	

A Woman Up a Tree (pages 24–28)

1. A. She wanted to save it from being cut down.

2. F. "Here I can be the voice and face of this tree."

3. B. Lumber companies promised not to cut it down.

4. D. The author believes that saving the tree is a good thing.

5. A. She managed to protect the tree.

6. C. to show what the tree looks like

7. I feel inspired. I feel angry. I feel hopeful. Responses will vary, but should include words from the text that support the emotion stated.

8.

Who	Julia Hill
Did What	lived in a redwood tree for 2 years
When	1997-1999 (these years can be inferred from the article)
Where	northern California
Why	to protect Luna from being cut down

The Coral Reef Crisis (pages 29–33)

1. D. Most coral reefs may die in 20 years.

2. C. to tell readers about the troubles coral reefs face

3. E. "Scientists are worried about the world's coral reefs."

4. A. Ocean water is getting warmer.

5. C. concern

6. A. to show the dangers facing coral reefs

7. seems like rock/has a stone-like surface made up of tiny clear animals; polyps stick together to form colonies as the colonies grow; they form reefs; they depend on algae (tiny sea plants)

8. Students should base their summaries on evidence from the text.

Answer Key *(cont.)*

Undersea Volcanoes (pages 34–38)

1. A. "They are deep under the sea."

2. B. the seam on a baseball

3. D. Lava builds up layers of rock.

4. C. the Mid-Ocean Ridge

5. E. "It is almost 500 miles wide." G. "It's more than 30,000 miles long."

6. A. At one time, the Hawaiian islands did not exist.

7. The Mid-Ocean Ridge is the largest mountain range on Earth, but few people have seen it. It's hundreds of mountains and volcanoes are located deep under the sea. The Mid-Ocean Ridge is more than 30,000 miles long and nearly 500 miles wide.

8. Answers may vary, but should be similar to:
   - An underwater volcano on the Mid-Ocean Ridge erupted off the coast of Iceland.
   - It spilled lava, which cooled.
   - As more lava flowed, layers built up.
   - The mountain of lava broke through the sea's surface in 1963.
   - Lava kept flowing until 1967, making Surtsey grow bigger.

She Gives Them Food for Thought (pages 39–42)

1. B. It takes place in a garden.

2. C. how to grow food

3. E. "Waters helps the kids to grow carrots, strawberries, and other food."

4. D. Waters is doing something new and different.

5. C. Waters does not think chemicals should be used on food.

6. C. Waters enjoys growing food in the garden.

7. The article states that science, art, math, and social studies classes take place in the garden. "Their science class takes place in a garden. The students use the garden for more than science class. Math, art, and social studies lessons are also taught there."

8. Accept any four: how to grow vegetables, how to eat healthy, how to make healthy meals, how to grow food without harmful chemicals, how to care for a garden

For Sale: Rare and Stolen Pets (pages 43–47)

1. D. stolen

2. G. "Often poor people steal rare animals from the wild."

3. B. They are endangered.

4. C. Don't buy rare and endangered animals for pets.

5. A. They would no longer be stolen and smuggled.

6. A. The chimp will be free.

7. It is a bad idea to buy a rare pet. "Many of these animals are rare or endangered." They should be allowed to live in their natural homes. They do not want to be pets. "Wild animals do not make good pets. They bite. They wreck homes and belongings. Even with loving owners, they die from not having the right food or environment."

8. **What is the problem**? Rare animals are being sold as pets.

   How can it be solved? People need to stop buying rare animals.

   Who? People who need money.

   Where? They steal the animals from their homes.

   Why? They sell the animals.

Answer Key *(cont.)*

Threads of Kindness (pages 48–51)

1. A. a company where clothes are made
2. C. They are able to get jobs.
3. F. "She used to worry about finding a good job."
4. B. around a lake
5. D. It is wonderful to help people.
6. A. Tran teaches teenagers to sew in a classroom.
7. Answers will vary; possible adjectives are noted in boldface:

   Tran is **talented** because he can sew and teaches other people how to sew. He is **kind, caring, thoughtful**, and **helpful** because he wanted to help the girls. He is **hard-working** since he runs a center for disabled children, and he is **generous** because he invested $1,500 of his own money.
8.

Problem Before Meeting Tran	How the Problem Was Solved
1. They didn't have jobs.	1. He taught them a skill so they got jobs.
2. They had no money.	2. The jobs let them earn money.
3. They felt sad and hopeless.	3. They felt happy and hopeful.

The Long Trail (pages 52–55)

1. D. a dog
2. F. "The snow and ice hurt Buck's paws."
3. B. Buck and the other dogs will keep going even though they are tired.
4. C. hopeful
5. A. Surviving in the Yukon is not easy.
6. A. to show how sled dogs work
7. Answers will vary, but may include: tired, cold, overworked, determined to keep going, sore, aching, in need of sleep, exhausted, weary, wishing to escape. For example:

   I feel tired and cold. We have been running for days. Even though I am overworked, I am determined to keep going. I hope that soon I can rest my sore paws and get some sleep.
8. Accept any four: cold feet; sore feet; limping; aching paws; aching shoulder; tired

Paul Bunyan (pages 56–59)

1. B. They move to Minnesota so he can have more space.
2. D. a folktale
3. B. They are both very big.
4. D. Babe grows so large it is hard to imagine.
5. G. "It took a whole day for a bird to fly from one of his horns to the other!"
6. C. to show how much bigger Paul and Babe are compared to everything else
7. The story is fictional because no human being could do the things in the story. First off, storks delivered Paul to his parents. As an infant, Paul drank the milk of 24 cows every day. Paul turns over on his raft and causes a tidal wave in the ocean. Paul destroys forests when he rolls around in his sleep. No ox could be as large as Babe, either. Babe eats 30 bales of hay as a snack. It takes a whole day for a bird to fly from one of his horns to the other. Babe is blue, too. The lakes in Minnesota are formed by water filling Paul and Babe's footprints.
8. The Venn diagram may include the following:

   • Baby Paul: drinks milk from 24 cows, eats 10 barrels of porridge in one meal, sleeps on a raft in the ocean, causes a tidal wave when he rolls over, destroys forests when he rolls over

   • Typical Baby circle: drinks a few bottles of milk, eats a small amount of food, sleeps in a cri

   • Intersection of circles: have parents, drink milk, eat food, take naps

Answer Key *(cont.)*

Go Fly a Kite! (pages 60–64)

1. B. discover something new about the world

2. D. Everybody in the city knows him.

3. F. "I knew where Ben Franklin lived—everyone in Philadelphia did."

4. C. "An electric spark jumped from the key to his fingers."

5. G. to tell a famous story from a different point of view

6. A. how men and boys dressed at that time

7. Ezra is glad that his key was needed for the experiment. "I glowed with pride when Ben exclaimed, 'You have saved the day, young man!'" Then he feels foolish that he could not get into his house. "I had helped unlock a secret of nature—but I couldn't unlock my front door!"

8.

How Does Ezra Feel About Ben Franklin?	How Do You Know?
1. Ezra admires Ben Franklin.	1. Ezra says he forgot his key because he was so excited about seeing "Philadelphia's greatest citizen, Benjamin Franklin."
2. Ezra is curious about Ben Franklin.	2. Ezra hid outside his house and followed him because "I knew he was up to something, and I wanted to watch the genius at work."

A Bedouin Tale (pages 65–69)

1. B. to teach a lesson

2. C. caring

3. E. "He stopped the many tribes from fighting one another."

4. A. It helps the reader to understand that the sons were selfish. B. It helps the reader to understand that the father wants the sons to work together. E. It helps the reader to understand that the father cares about his sons.

5. G. "His three sons, Yusef, Zaid, and Omar, argued about who should take charge if their father died." H. "You see, my sons, each stick is easy to break on its own, but together, they are stronger."

6. D. to show how hard the brothers tried to prove their strength

7. Abu Yusef gives his sons a challenge of breaking sticks to teach them that they are weaker as individuals than they are as a team that works together. "'You see, my sons, each stick is easy to break on its own, but together, they are stronger. The same is true for you,' Abu Yusef said." OR "The brothers understood their father's message: Alone, each son was weak, but together, they were strong."

8. Accept any four: courageous, fair, peacekeeper, clever, wise, ill, upset

Answer Key *(cont.)*

The Lion and the Wild Boar (pages 70–73)

1. A. They will fight until one dies.

2. C. Sometimes we have good reason to work with those we do not like.

3. E. "Enemies will unite against a common enemy."

4. B. meaning 2

5. D. "Those buzzards will eat whoever loses our battle."

6. B. They know that they will die without water. C. They do not want to be eaten by the buzzards.

7. The lion has the better argument because he is the king of the wild beasts. The wild boar should wait his turn. OR The wild boar has the better argument because he got there first. The lion should wait his turn.

8. The Venn diagram may include the following:

   • Lion circle: can roar, has sharp teeth, has big paws with claws

   • Wild Boar circle: has sharp tusks, has hooves

   • Intersection of circles: thirsty, angry, proud, stubborn, tired, afraid of buzzards

Racing a Tornado (pages 74–78)

1. C. fear

2. F. "The driver looked as frightened as we felt."

3. A. to show just how close the tornado was B. to show the size of the tornado

4. D. suspense

5. C. huge

6. A. "Maria screamed and pointed, 'There's a tornado!'" B. "The woman at the wheel rolled down the side window and shouted, 'Get in!'"

7. The narrator calls the tornado a monster because she is terrified. The twister seemed like a living thing that is coming after the children. "The driver looked as frightened as we felt." "The black, twisting funnel seemed to be chasing us." "A roaring like a freight train passed over us." "We had survived—barely." "That was a race we didn't ever want to run again!"

8. Beginning: The kids went for a bike ride and had a picnic.

   • Middle: A tornado came roaring toward them, and a driver took them in her car.

   • End: They hid under a bridge and were saved when the tornado passed right over them.

The Treasure Hunt (pages 79–83)

1. B. hopeful; D. smart

2. A. disappointed

3. H. "There's no treasure here—just a lot of books."

4. C. when they are at the library

5. A. There are different kinds of treasures.

6. C. to show that they tell the librarian that they found the treasure

7. We think in words. Words let us say what we think and communicate ideas to others. We cannot make progress without words. "Without words, we couldn't say what we think and feel. We couldn't create ideas. Words let us move forward together."

8. Sunshine Bank, City Hall, Paws Pet Store, the public library

It's a Dog's Life (pages 84–88)

1. A. He thinks Butch really loves him. B. He can hear Butch's thoughts.

2. D. He only wants to play for a short time.

3. F. "Doesn't he ever get tired of this game? I know I do."

4. D. crazy

5. C. to show that dogs do not always think what we expect

6. C. to illustrate part of the action in the story

7. 2—Andy can hear Butch's thoughts.

   1—Andy feels Butch lick his face.

   5—Butch is upset that he cannot have human food.

   3—Andy takes Butch to the park.

   4—Butch talks to dogs at the park.

8. When Andy realizes he can hear his dog's thoughts, he is *shocked* and *excited*. He is *surprised* to learn that Butch doesn't enjoy the fetch as much as Andy thought he did. Andy feels *discouraged* when he hears Butch call him "okay for a human." He thought Butch really loved him.

Answer Key (cont.)

Windy Nights (pages 89–92)

1. C. the movement of air
2. B. trees
3. H. "Whenever the trees are crying aloud"
4. B. back and forth
5. A. gallop
6. D. the wind
7. The author describes a windy night as "a man goes riding by." He uses the word *gallop* to let the reader know that the wind is a man galloping on a horse. The fast pace of the horse creates the wind current. "Why does he gallop and gallop about?" "By on the highway, low and loud, by at the gallop goes he." The writer also states, "By at the gallop he goes, and then by he comes back at the gallop again."
8. Accept any four rhyming pairs: set/wet; high/by; out/about; aloud/loud; sea/he; then/again

A Pleasant Day (pages 93–96)

1. C. "For the sun shines bright today"
2. A. happiness
3. G. "Everything is laughing, singing"
4. A. nice
5. A. "See the kittens, full of fun" C. "Birds and brooks and flowers see" D. "All the pretty flowers are springing"
6. D. "For it is a pleasant day"
7. This poem makes me long for a sunny day. The words the author uses to make me feel this way include *pleasant, happy, laughing, fun,* and *merry.* Accept any supported response.
8. laughing, singing, talking OR laugh, sing, talk

The Plumpuppets (pages 97–100)

1. A. a fairy
2. C. to make children comfortable so they fall asleep
3. F. "They plump up the pillow, all soft, cool, and fat,"
4. C. meaning 3
5. D. fluffing up a pillow
6. B. "The little Plumpuppets are those I love best."
7. They are called plumpuppets because they "plump up" pillows.
8. Accept any four: plump up pillows, watch sleepyheads, turn down sheets, tuck children in bed, dance on pillows, wish children goodnight

Mr. Macklin's Jack O'Lantern (pages 101–104)

1. C. joy and fright
2. A. pulls down the blind
3. D. They laugh.
4. A. The room gets dark and Mr. Macklin lights a candle.
5. G. "Then all the inside dark is made as spooky and as horrorful"
6. D. to show what Jack looks like
7. 5—He lights a candle inside the pumpkin.

   2—He carves eyes and a nose.

   4—He puts his pipe into the pumpkin's mouth.

   1—He gets a knife.

   3—He carves thirteen teeth.
8. Everyone in the tool-house asks Mr. Macklin "where's the door?" They do it because they want to escape. Once the Jack O'Lantern is lit, it looks spooky with its face reflected and flickering on the walls of the shed. "Then all the inside dark is made as spooky and as horrorful as Halloween, and creepy crawl the shadows on the tool-house floor."

Notes

Notes

Notes